D1371906

RESUCCEED

Create an Extraordinary Future
While You Sleep by Using the
5-Minute Epic Evening Ritual

JAMES COLBURN

RESUCCEED

Create an Extraordinary Future
While You Sleep by Using the
5-Minute Epic Evening Ritual

JAMES COLBURN

FREE FAST LAUNCH PACKAGE

GIVE OR GET THE GIFT OF RESUCCEEDING

Whether you're curious about *Resucceed* but not quite ready to make the investment or you would like to encourage someone you love and care for to check it out, I've created a totally FREE way for you to do just that.

Readers find the Resucceed system and the 5-Minute Epic Evening Ritual such a transformational process that they want to share it with those they love and care for. To help, I have created what I call the "Free Fast Launch Package," which you can obtain by visiting www.jamescolburn.net/resources. By selecting the "Free Fast Launch Package," you can send you or your friends and loved ones the following for FREE:

- Three chapters of *Resucceed: Create an Extraordinary Future While You Sleep by Using the 5-Minute Epic Evening Ritual*

- FREE 5-Minute Epic Evening Ritual PDF Checklist

- FREE Training Videos and Audio on how to implement and immediately begin to Resucceed today.

Enjoy,

James

A SPECIAL INVITATION TO JOIN THE RESUCCEED COMMUNITY

L ike-minded fans and readers of *Resucceed* make up the extraordinary community that has put to work the daily transformational practice of the 5-Minute Epic Evening Ritual. As the creator of the Resucceed success ritual, I feel it is my responsibility to create and maintain an online opportunity to share, connect, and engage as a community with those who have learned and benefited from the art and design of asking great questions just five minutes before bedtime.

It is my hope and dream that those who find the Resucceed 5-Minute Epic Evening Ritual beneficial will become members of our growing community to inspire and support one another and provide accountability within the online community for transformational growth.

Just go to Facebook and type "The Resucceed Community" (or visit www.theresucceedcommunity.com) and request to join the Resucceed Community on Facebook®. There you will be able to connect with like-minded individuals who are in the process of practicing the Resucceed success ritual.

I'll be moderating the Resucceed Community on Facebook personally and checking in regularly to provide feedback, encouragement, and support. It is my honor to be a part of the Resucceed Community.

If you'd like to connect with me personally on social media, follow @James_Colburn on Twitter and Facebook.com/james. colburn on Facebook. Please feel free to send me a direct message, leave a comment, or ask me a question. I do my best to respond to each message. Let's connect soon!

If you'd like to set up a personal 15 minute phone call with me, simply go to www.jamescolburn.net/coaching and follow the prompt to "Schedule a FREE 15-Minute Call." From there you will be directed to my scheduling application.

DEDICATION

To my beautiful and wonderfully patient wife, Maurita, and our three children, Eliot, Lucas, and Madeline. Without your support, *Resucceed* would be just another neat idea. I love you all far more than I could ever put into words.

To my mom and dad, who insisted I dream the dream and never give up on that dream.

This book is dedicated in loving memory of my dad,
Nordahl Nelson Colburn.

THE RESUCCEED MISSION

Transform Five Million Lives by Asking Great Questions
Just Five Minutes before Bedtime

In addition to donating a percentage of the profits from each copy of *Resucceed* sold to non-profit charities, including Family Lines and Medical Teams International, thousands of copies of *Resucceed* are donated each year to hospitals, schools, fundraisers, and other organizations and individuals that are in desperate need of inspiration and transformation. Our mission is to get *Resucceed* in the hands of 5,000,000+ people so that we can Transform Five Million Lives by Asking Great Questions Just Five Minutes Before Bedtime. Please enjoy and share this book often with those you love.

www.medicalteams.org

www.familylines.org

CONTENTS

SECTION III: RE-ENGAGE

SECTION IV: RE-AFFIRM

FOREWORD

Resucceed is a special book for me, and writing this foreword holds special meaning. James and I were introduced by mutual friends. Drawn together by our mutual zeal for human potential, the art of daily disciplines, and connecting with people who insist on making a difference while here on earth, we became friends quickly. When James asked if I would write the foreword for *Resucceed*, I didn't hesitate to think about it because I feel strongly that *Resucceed* is the next-level success handbook for the already successful.

As the author of *The Miracle Morning*, I believe in daily rituals that harness the best self-improvement practices and propel individuals to personal, professional, and financial success. Your morning routine and getting up when you *choose to*, rather than when you *have to*, create not only the difference between massive success and simply getting by, but also the difference between fulfillment and success without meaning.

Evenings are the key to mornings because the path to becoming a morning person starts at night. A great morning begins with setting your intentions right before you go to sleep. We know from experience that the last thought you have before you close your eyes at night is the first one that arises in the morning. This is, in part, why you can bound out of bed on the day you leave for vacation but find it hard to do so for regular life.

The bedtime ritual of the resucceed system prepares you for optimal sleep and helps you take advantage of that time to answer great questions, the answers to which come through in miraculous ways. Being mindful, grateful, and inquisitive as you fall asleep will help you wake up ready to be your best self and pursue success accompanied by meaning and fulfillment.

Join me in taking the resucceed challenge to add the 5-Minute Epic Evening Ritual to your daily success routine. I believe you will find that the power of asking great questions and tapping into the creative mind and the miraculous transformational.

Here's to your re-success!

Hal Elrod

#1 best-selling author, *The Miracle Morning*
(MiracleMorningBook.com)

INTRODUCTION

COULD THIS BOOK BE FOR YOU?

Miracles are a retelling in small letters of the very same story which is written across the whole world in letters too large for some of us to see.

—C.S. LEWIS

You will know right away if this book is for you because these first few pages will either resonate with you and your experience so far in life or they won't. I'm pretty sure you are in the right place if you are an already-successful individual who has achieved great things, both professionally and financially, but there are times when you feel a nudge or hear a whisper that reminds you that you are destined for more than you are currently doing, becoming, or settling for.

In those moments, you desire to feel complete, to experience more fulfillment in your success, and find meaning in what you do. Ultimately, you want to feel alive, and often your achievements, though extraordinary by conventional standards, fall short for you and leave you looking for more. Even if you don't know what variety of *more* you seek, the itch remains.

I've heard an actual voice many times around 2:00 a.m. when my house is quiet and still. It happened often enough for me to form a routine: I heard it, and then I tried to ignore it. The voice challenges me and says, "Seriously, you're going to settle for survival success." Sound familiar?

Your experience might be different: a passing feeling, a thought on the way to and from work, or a message when you're on vacation. You'll know this book is for you because the yearning for more always returns, even if you've avoided taking action and maybe hoped it would go away.

You might even feel guilty for wanting more than your current brand of success. I mean, for many, that success is the envy of others—their family, their friends, the people in their neighborhood. But it's not enough for you.

And all this said, the desire for meaning and fulfillment may disappear from time to time, when life gets busy or you experience a surge of achievement in your life. But the voice, that thought, the longing always returns—especially at inopportune moments.

If this sounds familiar, I have some good news and bad news for you. The good news is I have discovered a way to stop the whispers in the middle of the night and the disruptive thoughts in the day. I've learned how to transform every area of my life *while I sleep*. And the great news is you can too! It's easy. How could it not be? Like I said, it all happens while you sleep. I call this system the 5-Minute Epic Evening Ritual. The result is resucceeding and a life of fulfillment and purpose.

The bad news is that, to take advantage of this system and resucceed while you sleep, you must, like I did, face some hard truths and ditch the lies you tell yourself. In short, you've got to get disgusted with your norm!

A couple more things about resucceeding you should know: The hurdles we put in the way of living a life of fulfillment that comes from resucceeding are real, but it turns out, we are the ones who put them there. We prop up excuses about why we can't resucceed right now, like, "There's too much risk" or "I'll do it when I retire" or "After the kids finish school" or "When we have fewer bills to pay" or "I'm too old to reinvent." Not knowing where to start or how to go about resucceeding is a challenge, but I will help you with that.

The resucceed candidate knows that they are designed for much more, called to be more, and pulled to take action. Is this you? Are you looking for a practical step-by-step system to show you how to authentically resucceed? Then welcome, this book is for you.

Before we get started, I want to tell you a little about me and the journey of writing this book. This process was a huge part of my own resucceed adventure. If I'm honest, writing this book was exhausting. You should know I don't consider myself an author. This project was more like a responsibility, a life call. At the start, I had grandiose plans of effortlessly and eloquently spilling words onto paper. Well, that didn't happen. Sure, I had moments of self-proclaimed brilliance, but those were rare.

Instead, it went more like this: I'd write a sentence, read the sentence, delete the sentence, shout an expletive or two under my breath so that the kids wouldn't hear (most of the time), and then repeat. That went on for a few years. I've written this book four times. You read that right—four times. Each version was slightly different, but with each iteration arrived more of the essence, my truth, and the heart of what I was trying to say.

First, I struggled to start the book. A battle raged in my head with a voice that claimed I was not enough for the project: not smart enough, not good enough, I didn't know enough. You name it—not enough. Period. Once I got a good start and felt like I was in the zone, I became terrified of finishing. Reaching the end meant sending the book out into the world, which was a lot more uncertain than writing it, and writing it had been massively uncertain.

Also, I had hoped to leave my personal stories out of the book. You know, I'd simply be the reporter on the subject while never having to be transparent or go deep into my own struggles with success or what it means to me to authentically resucceed.

I imagined throwing in some of my opinions here and there, but I had no plan to tell you about the obstacles I faced or relive anything as part of writing this book.

No such luck here. This might explain why I had to write the book four times, the fourth version being the most transparent of them all. I learned quickly that, to resucceed, we must show up in our story. Turns out that writing a book and attempting to keep myself out of the story, well, that goes directly against the resucceed system as I learned the hard way.

One of the biggest hurdles in writing this book was my attempt to define success and achievement accurately. I quickly realized a one-size-fits-all definition doesn't exist because success is a moving target for us all and each of us views it differently. My lack of clarity meant certain aspects of earlier versions of the book were too vague. I remember how I sometimes sounded like a Greek philosopher, carelessly sharing my energetic delusions regardless of whether they would make sense or be helpful to anyone. I've worked hard to limit this for you.

As I typed and talked with others about my writing, I began to understand that my tendency toward the confusing and vague was often a smokescreen or perhaps a subconscious tactic I used to keep myself out of the story.

This felt like my breaking point at first but became more of a breakthrough over time for me and my resucceeding journey. I realized that vagueness had plagued me my entire life and that my success and even my view of resucceeding was unclear, so I couldn't explain it with precision.

Funny, I now understand that it was in writing this book that I discovered two of the most important components of resucceeding. First, I needed to include my own story. Second, I needed to get specific. It turns out that many people just like me struggle with the same issues in their own successes, their own achievements. More often than not, our success and achievement is missing, in a word, *us*. Our success and achievement have eclipsed us. We disappear from our story and confuse who we are with our success and achievement; they overshadow us. And the worst part? We allowed it.

Could this book be for you? Only you know for sure. But if you have made it this far, then at least a small part of you knows you are destined for more than your current brand of success and achievement. I'm so glad you're here.

Before we begin the journey to resucceed, I have a few promises to make to you.

PROMISES

I've always thought anyone can make money.
Making a life worth living, that's the real test.

—ROBERT FULGHUM

Since this book is for successful, high achievers like you, I imagine you are a lot like me in certain ways. But, though it's hard to pin down, it's important that you understand what it means to be successful or a high achiever.

Success and achievement come in many sizes and varieties, and they aren't always about money. This book is written for the successful achiever as defined by you. Whether you are financially successful, a successful parent, an amazing volunteer—you name it, if you believe you have enjoyed a certain level of success and achievement, whatever that might be—this book is for you.

My guess is that you are extremely busy, and the last thing you want is another self-help book on success or a bunch of happy quotes on the topic. Instead, what you want is a clear and precise approach to help you reclaim meaning and passion, to resucceed in your life and career. You want to define it, move toward it, and acquire it. And I bet you're super curious about how all this can start while you sleep.

Understanding this about you, I have three promises I want to make.

PROMISE #1: I WILL NOT WASTE YOUR TIME.

I love Robert Fulghum's books. You might remember his most popular book, *All I Really Need to Know I Learned in Kindergarten*. I loved them all. They were small books with short, powerful stories about life, many of which were drawn from Fulghum's personal experience. He wrote as if his memory were a filmstrip he felt bound to share because of the lessons contained within. He never claimed to be an expert on the lessons, but he observed situations, gained wisdom, and put all of this into words.

When I read Fulghum's books, I felt as if I were going on short trips in my head with him where I could glean a little and then step back into my life and put into practice some of what I learned.

So it is with my intention for this book.

Since resucceeding means doing things differently, evolving and becoming, it is natural to resist it. Steven Pressfield explained the mechanism this way: "The more important a call or action is to our soul's evolution, the more resistance we will feel toward pursuing it." You know this is important, or you wouldn't invest your valuable time reading this book. Understand that a part of you will try anything to get out of it.

I'm hoping these brief trips will help reduce your resistance. This book is shorter than many, easy to read, and contains highly actionable but bite-size chunks that allow you to make steady progress.

I hope you'll give yourself permission and space to take these short trips with me, one chapter at a time, to learn and grow and return to your life to apply the material. Not in one big splash, but incrementally, day by day, week by week.

Even more importantly, this book teaches you how to tap directly into your creative mind through the subconscious and also the wonder of the divine miraculous for answers to your great questions, those questions you don't yet know to ask. Resucceeding allows you the necessary space to break free from resistance and achieve your new brand of success and achievement that includes fulfillment, meaning, and joy—all in manageable increments of time. As Bill Gates said, "Most people overestimate what they can do in one year and underestimate what they can do in ten years." Take this one step at a time.

PROMISE #2: I WILL SHOW YOU HOW.

I promise to provide you with helpful information and specific steps. I understand the busy lives successful people lead, so I've included Quick Takeaways at the end of each chapter to apply what you've learned to your real life immediately without the need for pen and paper or a quiet room to contemplate. I want you to have concrete ways to resucceed within each chapter right away, not after you've finished the book or can wrap your mind fully around the concept. This book offers a clear focus on a simple, winning resucceed system that I have created and use in my own life and that I'm sharing with you now. Here is what you will find.

In section 1, I share my resucceeding journey and how I developed the 5-Minute Epic Evening Ritual that allows me to use my sleep to access the wisdom that was otherwise inaccessible to me. In chapter 1, you'll learn the definition of resucceeding and how the call to change might show up in your life. In chapter 2, I share how I personally received the message to resucceed. Chapter 3 will help you understand the difference between a life of success and a life with success and fulfillment. Next comes chapter 4, where I tell you exactly what it will take for you to make the decision to resucceed by revealing what stands in your way. In chapter 5, you'll identify what you need to let go of and what you need to embrace after you make the decision to resucceed. In chapter 6, I lay out the main tool of the resucceed system, the bedtime routine that will allow you to change your life while you sleep, and in chapter 7, I reveal the power of productive sleep.

From there, you'll find separate sections to help you craft the questions that comprise the framework of the daily resucceed system. Section 2 is about re-assessing or intentionally taking stock of where you are each day and in your life as a whole. In chapter 8, I talk about language and how we speak to ourselves. In chapter 9, I help you assess how you manage your energy. Chapter 10 shows you how to step out of your comfort zone and reach for the stretch zone, which, of course, is where growth happens. In chapter 11, you'll meet your resistance, and in chapter 12, I encourage you to take time for Legos.

Section 3 is about re-engaging in your life. This section will help you prioritize the focus of your attention rather than being reactive or unnecessarily entranced by your current success and achievement. In chapter 13, I'll help you put first things first. Then we'll take time for reflection in chapter 14. Chapter 15 is all about *enoughness*, and chapter 16 covers the echoes we leave in the world. Finally, in chapter 17, I encourage you to digest, not merely consume, what you take in during the day.

Section 4 is about re-affirming in your life. I encourage you to celebrate great discoveries and relax into not having all the answers. In chapter 18, I focus on becoming. Then I discuss moments of brilliance in chapter 19 and the miraculous in chapter 20. I help you find gratitude in small things within chapter 21 and round out this section with celebrations in chapter 22.

I conclude the book with the epilogue, where I encourage you to celebrate the unfinished nature of our resucceed adventure in what I call the unfinished melody of our lives.

PROMISE #3: I WILL BE REAL WITH YOU.

I promise to be reflective and transparent with you. I share my story because it might resonate with you, and I want you to see precisely how this system worked for me. But I also will be reflective: I will reveal what the events of my life meant to me and how I responded to them and applied the resucceed system. I include the messy stuff because I want you to know I'm serious; I have struggled with this too. Our stories may not be the same, but my hope is that you will be able to follow my example to reflect on and be honest with yourself about your life. That's what I want for you. And that's why I will be real with you. I want to go deep, and I want you to give yourself the space to do the same. To authentically resucceed requires this, and since you're reading this book, I figure you're up for it.

Are you ready for a new brand of success? Are you ready to resucceed in your life and career? The first thing you need to do is recognize the call to resucceed.

SECTION I

CHAPTER 1

RESUCCEED—THE CALL

*Take your victories, whatever they may be,
cherish them, use them, but don't settle for them.*

—MIA HAMM

What's in front of your eyes? I mean, what do you see that is obvious to you and probably to many of the people who know you? Perhaps your appearance when you look in the mirror, your relationships, your possessions, your symbols of success. Dig a little deeper, and you will find your skills, responsibilities, achievements, and even your debts. Your past is there too.

In front of our eyes we find the tangible and intangible people, places, and things that determine how we define ourselves, make decisions, and consume our hours, days, and years. What's in front of our eyes is often worthy and honorable (our relationships), sometimes valiant (our achievements), and this is often how we measure our progress in life.

For most people, this is quite possibly the beginning and end of the story. In effect, we come, we conquer and acquire the visible, and then we pass away. The resulting eulogy consists of sweet praise and an appreciation for a life well lived, for a soul who went big and then went home. And again, in front of our eyes, things would look pretty good, even at our memorial service. We convince ourselves that we have arrived with purpose, meaning, and true fulfillment when often what we are doing is keeping and maintaining ill-constructed avatars of ourselves.

It makes sense to me that we settle for this. The cultural pressure to obtain and then receive praise for the acquisition of stuff, better stuff, different stuff is wonderfully seductive. Our brains treat this as a win, and it is much easier to focus on and celebrate the obvious and visible than to explore what lies within us, the invisible. But I believe there is more to life than meets the eye, and to find it, resucceeding is required.

At the risk of mentioning an older (though popular) movie, I'm reminded of the Steve Martin movie *The Jerk*. You might remember when Navin Johnson enters a phone booth and starts looking through a phone book. When he finds his name, he screams with excitement, "I'm somebody now!"

Is it okay that we are somebody only because of the things we have constructed or by what we have achieved and can do successfully? By name only? Perhaps the example in the movie is extreme, but it highlights a subtler condition: We identify

with and measure our worth according to what is outside us—
the name assigned to us, our title, our past achievements and
success—but rarely by who we really are, from the perspective
of the heart. I challenge this notion and argue that what
makes us "somebody" is what lies within us that we so often
are desperate to reveal to others. It is our job to bring *that*
somebody forward. To integrate our essence with our visible
success and achievement *is* really our *something*.

If we should risk looking behind the obvious and deeper
into ourselves, we will find a larger and more profound purpose
for our lives, the invisible that begs to be made visible. It
won't be as overt as a billboard or a precise outline provided
by someone else. Fulfillment is not a product you can buy for
$199.99 or $199,999. Your purpose and value is a journey, and
you find it by being willing to look behind your eyes. As Simon
Sinek eloquently put it, "People don't buy what you do, they
buy why you do it." I like to say that fulfillment is the reason
behind the reason we do things.

Simply put, the journey you take reveals the *why* of *what*
you do in life. The journey is not a single road that trails off
in the distance, gently following the contours of the land. It
is one that moves from invisible to visible, one dusty road
and intersection at a time, and is mostly full of potholes and
unpaved sections that inspire growth and contribution, not
through ease and perfection. It is through our life challenges
that we grow. You've heard it before, but I'd like you to consider
again that the destination is not the goal—it's that we traveled
the road.

Each year we get a little older. I haven't surprised you there.
But, unfortunately, fraction by fraction, we become more
invisible. Not just to others, but also to ourselves. Buckminster
Fuller, a past Mensa president and renowned twentieth century

inventor, once suggested, "Ninety-nine percent of who you are is invisible and untouchable."

I remember my 80-year-old father would wear a baseball cap with the name of a famous World War II ship whenever he would go in public. One day I asked him why he always wore that hat.

"Squire," he said, calling me by my childhood nickname, "the older I get, the more invisible I am. When I wear this hat, I am no longer invisible. People come up to talk to me, shake my hand. They notice that I am here." Perhaps his version of being "somebody."

That moment was a clue on my resucceed journey, though I didn't put it all together just then. Resucceeding is about choosing to make the subtle and invisible parts of ourselves visible.

Ironically, although our purpose is initially unseen, it is easier to find than to maintain. Our culture and the demands of our success often drag us toward the pursuit of obvious, worldly achievements and away from the invisible road of our purpose and meaning. The world rejects prolonged focus on the invisible because the job at hand is always before us, always paramount, always begging for our attention. And with such pressures to perform and achieve, staying on the dusty, vague road of purpose and meaning often seems more like a chore than a blessing.

Undoubtedly, the road of purpose and meaning is peppered with distraction. When on the unmarked road, our ears and eyes are more alert, but this seems to attract roadblocks and diversions. Our humanness, if unchecked, wants to return to what is obvious, easier, and more comfortable (at least on the surface), instead of heeding the call we feel deep inside, the thing we are truly meant to be and do.

And then the midlife crisis appears. The midlife crisis is perhaps less of a crisis and more of an invitation, a pull to the invisible. And a midlife crisis doesn't happen neatly in the middle of our lives. But a day comes when dissonance emerges—from the gap between our purpose and what we've become—and produces extreme and noticeable discomfort. Usually found only in flashes on the periphery, in these intense moments, the deficit in what's in front of our eyes becomes clear. And though popularly attributed to men, both genders come to a place in life, an Ecclesiastes-type moment, when one wonders about the meaning in daily life: "'Meaningless! Meaningless!' says the Teacher. 'Everything is meaningless!'" (Ecclesiastes 12:8, NIV).

The lack of meaning can become a call to wake up rather than a dead end, though many who recognize this louder call choose to ignore it with bigger and bolder forays into known territory, the visible. Fearing what lies beyond their comfort zone, they pursue bigger goals and achievements, and in some cases, fall into even more destructive distractions. It's interesting (and tragic) what success we choose to settle for rather than to discover the truth of our purpose and what brings us joy and lasting fulfillment.

I am reminded of a friend I see once a year, normally in early January. He invites me to a coffee shop to catch up, and when he arrives, he approaches with a noticeable swagger. I immediately see the latest trappings of his success: fancy watch, cufflinks, and designer clothes. He offers to buy as he pulls out his designer wallet and drops it on the table as if it were a cinderblock brick. The content of our conversation usually focuses on the fact that, in his eyes, he is not making enough money. But he always has a plan, a New Year's resolution, that he believes will help him arrive at the wealth and material belongings he yearns for. Perhaps just around the corner he will feel like "somebody."

As I listen to my friend talk, I feel a little sick because I have been down the same road. I know how fragile and tender it is to be caught (lost) in the sham of achievement at the expense of losing myself.

Don't get me wrong: building wealth is not inherently bad. Wealth and material belongings alone are not the problem. We go astray when we assign our value and identity to building wealth and materialism with little thought to our wholeness.

This friend and most high achievers are lost in the fleeting nature of the pursuit of wealth—for the sake of wealth—with no plan for fulfillment or meaning. That is mistakenly reserved for another day. A day that, for many, never arrives. What a shame it would be to never go beyond that brand of success.

I came to the same place after acquiring what I considered to be significant financial success. I realized that achievement without fulfillment in my life was similar to building a house on sand. My lust for one-dimensional success, or what I call "survival success," bred horrible discontent in my life. I could never have enough money or material objects, and I knew deep inside that what goes up (my income) must come down. At the end of 2006, even as I celebrated the most successful year of my career up to that point, I was afraid of losing it all.

QUICK TAKEAWAY

Before you turn the page, ask yourself this question: what am I afraid of losing?

Is your answer about the visible, lived life you are enjoying, or is it about the invisible, unlived life you have deferred for later? What if your biggest fear were never revealing your unlived life?

I'm excited to tell you next about my Costco run on Christmas Eve that changed my life forever.

CHAPTER 2

MY PERSONAL CALL

*If we want to save our lives, we cannot cling to them
but must spend them with abandon.*

—PARKER J. PALMER

Late on Christmas Eve in 2006, I sat motionless on the comfortable futon couch in my waterfront vacation home and looked out at the still water just beyond our deck. I noticed a small surfacing rock just beyond the shoreline that had what seemed to be a small sapling growing out of it. If you had been observing this scene, you would have concluded I was living the dream.

This day marked the end of the most successful year of my sales career. I had broken every company sales goal, and our family income was greater than ever. We had gone to Hawaii twice and purchased two investment homes and new cars. We wanted for nothing. Well, that's not entirely true, but it sure looked that way.

Although we had always lived a simple life (from the outside looking in), I did not operate within a budget that year, though my wife, Maurita, probably did. I bought what I wanted whenever I wanted it. At the end of each month, there was always another big bucket of money to fill the checking account. Today, I write this with borderline disgust, but back then, I would have said this was the pinnacle of my sales career.

Sitting there watching the still water, I could hear my two boys playing with Lego bricks and race cars in their room. Maurita and her mother were cleaning up after dinner and prepping for the Christmas festivities. Little did anyone know that beneath my calm veneer lay an inferno of emotion, tension, and conflict.

My head felt like it was spinning out of control as thoughts of inadequacy clanked around. On the one hand, I was proud of my accomplishments, and on the other, I was scared to death of them. With my great success came the responsibility to keep it up.

Doubts and fear of failure crept in as I wondered why my phone wasn't ringing. *Surely I can do one more sale tonight. Please, phone ring. Please, phone ring.* One more sale for the year. I had a starched shirt hanging in my car, and I was ready and waiting for that call.

As the minutes passed and the phone didn't ring, I thought I would lose my mind. I was simply not okay with being still or feeling content.

I understood what had happened even though I didn't want to admit it: I had lost myself in my own success. I had confused my identity and purpose with what I was great at, what people celebrated me for, which had little or nothing to do with *me* and a whole lot to do with *what I did*.

I jumped off the couch at 8:35 p.m., grabbed my keys from the kitchen counter, and yelled over my shoulder, "I'll be back shortly."

Costco was close to our home, and I knew if I could get through the door before 9:00 p.m., they wouldn't kick me out.

I reached the store 20 minutes later and ran inside. I wasn't the only one there that night, but now that I think about it, everyone else was probably buying gifts for others. I wasn't thinking about that as I threw the first TV with DVD player I saw into my cart along with a handful of movies. Then I headed to the checkout stand.

I arrived home about an hour later, feeling proud of myself as I walked through the door with the box. *Christmas had come early. I'd saved the day with a TV and a pile of movies!*

You should know Maurita and I had not installed a TV at the lake house to promote quiet and the sense of being away when we were there. My mad dash to Costco was about to change that. I figured the TV with DVD player and some movies would get my mind off the fact that my phone was not ringing and the *inadequacy* of my success in 2006.

The kids emerged from their bedroom to see what Dad had bought.

My wife stared and said, "I thought we didn't want a TV here?"

"We didn't," I said as I plugged it into the wall. I ripped the cellophane wrapper from one of the DVDs and shoved in a Nicholas Cage movie called *World Trade Center.* I rationalized that it would be educational for my three- and six-year-old boys.

As the movie started and I got comfortable on the couch with a boy under each arm, my wife interrupted and said, "Oh no, not a movie about terrorism on Christmas Eve."

I looked at the remote, then at Maurita, and back at the remote again. I knew she had a point, but I needed to get my mind off things, and this, I thought, would do the trick. Reluctantly, okay maybe a little angrily, I turned off the TV and told the boys to jump in bed for stories.

After everyone was asleep and I had put all the assembled toys under the tree, I returned to the living room. I sat on the couch in the dark, staring out the window at the sparkle of Christmas lights dancing across the water. My heart filled with sadness, and I couldn't figure out why. I reminded myself of all the money I had made this year, and yet couldn't shake how empty I felt inside. Part of me was scared that I might not keep up the same pace in 2007. I mean, who could keep up that pace? A deeper part of me wondered why all this money and success didn't make me feel better about myself. *Shouldn't I feel great?*

I didn't have the answers that night but had a clear sense that I had equated my value and identity with the wrong thing. Christmas Eve 2006 became a defining moment for me, and the TV and stack of movies a metaphor for the one-dimensional person I had become. The fact was I had sought, chased, and achieved the success I dreamed of, but at the cost of losing myself. I realized at that moment that answering and responding to the call of my life was more important than the success I had chased.

QUICK TAKEAWAY

Everyone knows their call deep down inside. It's not a secret. It is what already-successful, highly achieved individuals resist most of the time. So, what are you resisting while you chase success and achievement? This is most likely your call. I had imagined that my call was like a puzzle I had to decode but always felt I didn't have enough time for the decoding process. What if I told you that you already know your call? Understanding that, what is your call?

It's one thing to have an epiphany or pivotal moment in your life when you realize your priorities are in need of correction. But what can you do after that? In the next chapter, I describe the difference between what I call survival success and resucceeding. Understanding the difference and identifying those areas of your life that are about survival will help you decide if you are a good candidate for resucceeding.

CHAPTER 3

SURVIVAL SUCCESS VS. RESUCCEEDING

People have enough to live by but not enough to live for:
they have the means but no meaning.

—VIKTOR E. FRANKL

A time comes in the lives of successful individuals when the worst thing that happens is they make a big paycheck. The big paycheck is like a set of shackles, and the success like prison. What is often missing is the fulfillment, passion, and joy within our success. We somehow trade the keys to such redeeming things to fill our wallets. This is what I call *Survival Success*.

Let's be honest, we weren't handed a life and career success manual at birth. Instead, most of us fumble and bumble through life. We pick up advice here and there, but rarely in relation to finding our purpose, or at least not in a form we can apply. Early in life, we started saying *yes* to a whole lot of things, some of which were good for us, some not. We raised our hands physically or mentally to a wide range of experiences and disciplines.

According to Ryan Holiday, author of *Ego is the Enemy,* "All of us regularly say yes unthinkingly, or out of vague attraction, or out of greed or vanity. Because we can't say no—because we might miss out on something if we did. We think that 'yes' will let us accomplish more, when in reality it prevents exactly what we seek. All of us waste precious life doing things we don't like, to prove ourselves to people we don't respect, and to get things we don't want."

As we say yes to things that aren't consistent with our purpose, little by little we become good at a few of those things. People celebrate us for what we do well, and of course, that feels good. We start to think our achievement is who we *are.* And life moves on.

Over time, we realize that we are great at a couple things, and if we're lucky, we get paid for them. That feels incredible, and so we keep doing it. As I said earlier, for most people, the story stops right there: Successful people start to believe that what they are great at and what they have achieved defines them. In defining themselves that way, they are lost in the ups and downs of their achievement. As if their achievement is their lifeblood, their essence, their purpose. But it doesn't have to end that way. You can choose to resucceed.

Resucceeding is for the group of highly successful achievers who know your current brand of success has fallen short and become one-dimensional and is in desperate need of an overhaul. But because you lack the manual for success *and* purpose, no matter how powerful the yearning for meaning and fulfillment, you don't know how to pursue meaning and fulfillment, pay the bills, and keep the parts of your lifestyle that aren't in conflict with who you are. What's more, you often feel guilty about the desire to resucceed. You might think, *other people envy my success and dream of being me.*

Here's the deal: Just because you excel at some skill or possess a certain ability doesn't mean that is why you are here on earth or what you should give your life to. That's the lie of success, the trap and enticement of achievement. We reach a point of failure when we mistakenly become better versions of our *achievement* instead of better versions of *ourselves.* I sure did that night at the lake house in 2006. I knew my success had come up short, but I had no idea how to change it. I had assigned my identity to my success, which meant that, without it, I would be nothing—I would come up short. Or so I thought.

Like I mentioned before, I call this survival success. It starts with believing the lies we tell ourselves. Our achievements and the bills we must pay are more important than becoming better versions of ourselves and living with purpose and fulfillment. We fall for this lie that the risks are too great. We need to understand that the lie isn't outside of us: We tell it to ourselves. Steven Pressfield said it best when he suggested, "It's one thing to lie to ourselves. It's another thing to believe it." Maybe the voice that speaks in favor of survival success never goes away completely, but resucceeding requires we stop believing the lies.

I remember when I was 21 and showing off the fact that I lived on $720 per month. The work I did then was a form of survival, but I didn't identify with it—I worked for my life after five o'clock. But soon, that changed.

You've probably heard the story that a frog in a kettle would jump out of boiling water but remain if the water were to start out cool and only gradually begin to boil. Whether that is true for frogs or not, it certainly is for me. Over time, it seemed as if my bills increased, the stakes got bigger, and my need to have a successful job became greater and meant more than ensuring I had a life after work, much less fulfillment, purpose, and joy. Perhaps it wasn't the stakes that got higher, but instead that I assigned my identity and worth to my work, my level of achievement, and then without noticing, I became lost in it all.

Success can warp our thinking so that we view a successful career as a means of survival, not in the traditional sense of the word, but survival of the avatar we hope to perpetuate. Sadly, in this case, we seek to save ourselves from the risks of showing up in life, the uncertainty of living our purpose as a new brand of success, and allowing the mystery of the miraculous and infinite to fill our daily lives.

It is because of my experiences and realizing that most successful and highly achieving people come to a similar spot in life that I felt compelled, duty bound even, to create a systematic step-by-step system to resucceed.

And let me be clear: Resucceeding is not about succeeding again at something new. You can find a book already out there for that. Several thousand probably, and there may be an app too. Resucceeding is also not about giving up your zeal for professional and financial accomplishments. We are wired for achievement in all forms and should embrace our whole selves.

Instead, resucceeding is what already-successful people do when they are sick and tired of being *only* successful at the expense of becoming invisible in their pursuit of professional and financial goals.

Resucceeding is a mindset shift that starts with a set of nighttime disciplines and routines to harness the incredible power of the creative and subconscious aspects of our minds along with access to the miraculous while we sleep. Those disciplines involve working with the three *REs* of resucceeding—re-assessing, re-engaging, and re-affirming—each evening before we go to sleep. This system is so simple and effective that, if you take the risk and open yourself up to it, you can't help but begin your own process of resucceeding while you sleep.

But, before anyone can resucceed, they must experience a critical moment of awareness. I call this the *get disgusted* moment, a time when you tell the *Truth* about and to yourself. This process of getting disgusted isn't about being hard or tough on yourself. It's not about bullying yourself into change, but rather getting real about where you are and where you want to go.

My friend and mentor, Hal Elrod, mentioned his own process of getting disgusted when I interviewed him for a podcast. He said he had asked himself, "Why not me?" when he noticed other people breaking sales goals, receiving huge financial rewards, and achieving beyond the norm. And then he realized, yeah, *why not me?* Nothing had prevented him from pursuing the same levels of achievement. In other words, he had been selling himself short and needed to reframe the question. You can't resucceed if you don't make a clear and definitive decision to do so, and that starts with getting real, getting disgusted, and then making a definitive decision.

If resucceeding is the next right step for you and you want a step-by-step plan to transform your life, then it's time to get disgusted.

QUICK TAKEAWAY

Consider which parts of your success are more like survival success. The area of your success that borders on requirement for the sake of the avatar you seek to maintain. Is there any part of your current success that feels more like survival than blessing?

How do you feel when you think about the places in your life where you engage in survival success?

Once you have identified where you engage in survival success, the show you desperately want or need to keep in place, it's time to get disgusted with your show. In the next chapter, I break down exactly what it means to get disgusted and show you the power of changing the image you have created for yourself.

Are you ready?

CHAPTER 4

GET DISGUSTED: BEHIND THESE EYES

The real voyage of discovery consists not in seeking new landscapes, but in having new eyes.

—MARCEL PROUST

When I tell you that you must get disgusted to resucceed in life, what I mean is that you must make the real problem visible to yourself. You must become acquainted first with the ways you identify *who you are* with the measure of your success. But then you need to recognize the consequences that flow from abandoning your quest for meaning, passion, and fulfilment because you fear the uncertainty of your unlived life. Getting disgusted is that moment of severe inner conflict when you have no idea what you will do, but you know you must do something different. I challenge you to resist the urge to run away and instead reveal the best parts of your invisible life and respond to your true purpose and calling.

In *The Slight Edge*, Jeff Olson describes his own moment of disgust: "For whatever reason, as happens in so many people's lives, I found myself staring squarely at a fork in the road, a point I now refer to as my *day of disgust*: that moment of impact we sometimes hit in our lives when we come smack face to face with our circumstances and, without having a clue to the what or how of it, make a decision to change."

To further my point, I recently watched *Rogue One*, a prequel to the original Star Wars series. In this episode, although several characters are imprisoned, only one complains of being in the prison.

A blind man responds quietly, "There is more than one prison. I think you carry yours wherever you go." I mention this because we each carry our own prison, and it is this prison we must get utterly disgusted with to resucceed.

This is what resucceeding requires. We must first get disgusted with our current (or past) circumstances, no matter how hard we've worked to attain or preserve them. Resucceeding requires that we get over *what we have done* to accomplish *what we have yet to do, become, achieve, and contribute.* For the already-successful high achiever, this is essential because we become masters at believing the lies we tell about our current or past success. Somehow we think our ultimate desire is survival success, even if we feel unfulfilled and know that something greater is out there for us.

We live in a world where every product has a version number that marks its spot in the lineage of a product line. Remember Windows 95? (I'm still trying to forget Windows 95!) So it is with our lives. We are not immune to version labels, but what's interesting is that most of our version labels are self-imposed. We might say "I'm old school" or "I'm not tech savvy" or "I'm young at heart" or "I don't have a head for figures." The list is long, but when we say these things, we become attached to them, and soon we become them. To get disgusted, it helps to understand which version you have claimed for yourself. Let me show you an example of what I mean.

I was sitting with one of my close friends on his back deck enjoying cigars to celebrate his 70th birthday. He seems younger than that, closer to my own, though he is some 25 years older than me. He told me what the strangest part about being 70 is for him.

"Behind these eyes, I'm still 18 years old." He went on to say, "The only thing that is different is that my body is 70. But behind these eyes, I notice the same hot girls who enter the room as you do, James."

We had a good laugh, but I was amazed he'd used "behind these eyes," the same words I had been working with in the context of resucceeding, our unlived lives, and the process of lifting ourselves out of invisibility. More importantly, I had discovered a key distinction between our *real* reality and our *self-imposed* reality.

In the book *New Psycho-Cybernetics,* Maxwell Maltz and Dan S. Kennedy suggest that the limits of our lives are like two boxes, one inside the other. The outer box has a bold black line that represents our actual limits. So the bold outer line might represent the reality of my friend's age. If he wanted to be a star college quarterback right now, it won't happen because of his age and condition. Our physical limitations are real, and the bold line of the outer box represents those limits.

The inside box, however, is a dotted line that signifies our self-imposed limits, the version number we accept. Maltz and Kennedy say we can affect, shape, and grow the box with the dotted line. The goal is to push this dotted line box as close to, if not overlapping with, the bold line of the outer box. This process requires, in part, getting disgusted with our self-imposed limits and version numbers. It turns out that our biggest competition becomes ourselves if you think about it.

Most of us who are high achievers pushed our dotted line out when we were younger as a part of achieving our initial success. It was through this stretching the lines of our inner box that we became successful. But once we reached that level, we stopped pushing on the box or at least pushing in certain areas of our lives.

If this is you and you are ready to take a fresh look at that inner box, then you are ready to resucceed. You must decide not to settle or tolerate the gap between the dotted line and the bold one though.

Tony Robbins, one of the most influential motivation speakers of our time, has said, "We get what we tolerate." To be more precise, I would say we get what we *choose* to tolerate. How you feel about something is a choice, and when you choose to get disgusted, you can stop tolerating what doesn't serve you and start living beyond your past or current achievement.

In my experience, you must get disgusted enough to create the energy to overcome your resistance. What are you resisting? What is the call you are denying?

As I think back on my call, I realize that its essence was to end the invisibility of my life and show up. This was not some half-baked dream but instead an overwhelming "*had to* do" before the day I would not wake up. It was that serious.

For you, it might not be this clear, but this often shows up when people are most disenchanted with their current life or career and deeply feel the lack of passion, meaning, and fulfillment. This disenchantment sets up the perfect opportunity to choose to resucceed.

In these moments, I challenge you to allow the strong feelings to wash over you and let them move you to a point of personal disgust, not with yourself but the life that holds no fulfillment for you. In doing so, the call takes shape. As that call arrives in full color, you can do nothing but make that definitive decision to resucceed.

You might think you must hit bottom and then rake yourself over the coals. Not at all. If you are already successful and simply want to upgrade your version number, you need to download a new version of you, like you would the latest operating system for your computer.

The resucceed system and the 5-Minute Epic Evening Ritual facilitate the new download in your life and move you from the version you are to the version you want to become. You have to get disgusted, but unlike a character in a movie, you don't have to wait for the all-is-lost moment.

The system for getting disgusted and deciding to resucceed, whether you have hit bottom or not, follows three key principles, which I discuss in the next chapter: adopt full color thinking, tap into the creative mind, and get rid of the lies.

> **QUICK TAKEAWAY**
>
> Think of an area in your current version of success where you have pushed the Maltz-Kennedy dotted line closer to the bold line. How did you do that? What did it take? How long has it been since you held yourself accountable for doing this in your life? What is one way you could do it today?

Getting disgusted isn't so bad, is it? In fact, it's kind of fun to throw out the old to make room for the new. Now that you have that in place, it's time for a new version download.

CHAPTER 5

THE DOWNLOAD

When your values are clear to you,
making decisions becomes easier.

—ROY E. DISNEY

After you've become disgusted with the parts of your life that aren't working for you, you're ready to download the next version of you. It may take time, probably longer than it takes to install a new operating system for your electronic devices. But the concepts are straightforward, and the plan to implement them is simple as you will see when you encounter the 5-Minute Epic Evening Ritual.

This download consists of three principles that describe what you must step out of (or let go of) and what you must step into (or embrace).

1. ADOPT FULL COLOR THINKING

The decision to get disgusted and transform your life won't come from a list on a yellow pad or a mental exercise assessing pros and cons. Instead, you must base your resucceed decision on full color, glossy photos. What do I mean by that? You must get the clearest picture of what it means *to you* to resucceed, including all its attributes. To know where you're going, it helps to hold a vivid image, like a photo in full color, in your mind. Many of us have settled for black and white thinking. With this approach, the mind's eye gazes upon something vague that resembles a cartoon rendering of the future. I've learned that if you want to move toward anything, you must turn your fictional rendering into as real an image as possible that includes every conceivable detail. The better we get at forming these photos, the more we can resucceed.

Most successful individuals are great at making decisions and pursuing goals, and these are great skills to have. But the process comes up short because it focuses on becoming successful and *what we need to do* to get there. This is what we let go of when we resucceed. Instead, embrace *who you will become,* and then create a full color, glossy picture of that in our mind.

For example, to resucceed it's not good enough to want to be a writer and know the steps required to write a book. You must push yourself to imagine who you will become, the full color example of what being a writer will do to bring fulfillment, passion, and meaning to your life and, more importantly, the lives of those around you.

A full color photo in your mind of what you desire for your life, including all the details of what it means in terms of your purpose, is what full color thinking is all about.

2. TAP INTO THE CREATIVE MIND

The second thing you must embrace is the art of tapping into your creative mind. Understand that your mind is far more creative than you give it credit for. You must give yourself the space to create a new version of success and achievement that employs the senses and attributes of the whole person you wish to become.

For many, the creative mind sits dormant as they pursue the more simplistic ease of survival success. They find a formula for success and rely upon it without considering how they might change their approach for greater fulfillment. They do what makes them successful over and over again, but not what cultivates passion and joy.

You must take risks and step outside your comfort zone by letting your creative mind drive. It holds the power to lead and direct you through inspiration to become who you need to be to resucceed. Your role is to listen and then respond. If you commit to the process, your resucceeding journey will unfold with access to the miraculous.

3. GET RID OF THE LIES

I do a fair bit of coaching around the resucceed system, and in doing so, I have accumulated examples of some of the most destructive and damaging lies that interrupt any chance of resucceeding. It is important to identify and release these lies up front because it isn't until you stop repeating them that you can begin.

My mother made it clear that there are two types of lies: white ones and red ones. Red lies, according to my mom, are the inexcusable ones that hurt others. She believed that white lies were less destructive because they hurt only ourselves. For example, I would tell her that I had studied enough for my spelling test or brushed my teeth when I hadn't. These white lies didn't change the world or directly hurt anyone but me. At least that's what I thought then.

I've come to understand that white lies are often as destructive as red lies—if not more so. Your character and beliefs are lost in the white lies you tell others and, more importantly, the ones you tell yourself. Lies become the grand excuses that hold you back from resucceeding in your personal life and career. I view them as a trap that gets triggered every time we attempt to take a positive step forward. It's hard to resucceed when you must stop and free yourself regularly. Put another way, it's hard to download a new operating system when you have a virus present.

Here are the top four lies I have observed while working with individuals as a resucceed coach. You must be prepared to step out of these lies if you want to authentically resucceed.

LIE #1: I'm doing better than most.

When we have achieved a certain level of success in life, it is easy to justify the lack of fulfillment by looking at other people's success. I've noticed that people who are fully engaged in survival success tend to keep people in their lives who are less successful (I've done this too). It allows them to cement the lie that their lives are better than most.

This is not only about financial success. You might have an amazing marriage, while your friends complain about their relationships and feel unhappy. They might even ask you for advice because of your obvious marriage success. It can feel good, on the surface, to have this all figured out.

Or, you might be a physically fit person who surrounds yourself with friends who have given up on exercise, diet, and self-care. You are surely better off than most, but are you fulfilled?

Being successful in different areas of your life doesn't mean you aren't ready to upgrade your operating system. Comparing your level of fulfillment to someone else's (in other words, comparing what you experience inside to another person's outward appearance) will not bring you the life you are meant to live or help you fulfill your purpose.

Resucceeding is contingent upon dropping the lie that you are doing better than most people because that's not the point. Instead, resucceeding has everything to do with desiring meaning and purpose in your life regardless of how you stack up against others. To truly and authentically resucceed, you need to reveal what has been kept invisible in your own life.

LIE #2: I'm not enough.

This lie is one I leaned on for years. I talk about this at length in chapter 15. Dropping it has made a huge difference for me. The truth is that you, me, and everyone is born *enough*. That's right. When you showed up, when you cried for the first time in the hospital, you weren't required to do anything to qualify as enough.

So how did we get turned around? Somewhere along the way, we replace the truth with a feeling or suspicion. Something happened or someone said something that gave rise to doubt. If the experience or words are repeated often enough, the doubt becomes belief. Then we move through life trying to prove our worth and think we can become enough if only we say and do the right things.

Here are two incidents from my childhood to illustrate what I mean. One day, I told my mother I wanted to be president of the United States, and I asked her what I needed to do to make it happen. She came up with an answer (I no longer remember what she said), and she finished by saying, "You could do that if you wanted to." That felt wonderful, and though that wish passed, I'll never forget the warm and positive feelings that flowed from her belief that I was enough to be president.

Another time, I found my mother crying while she hung laundry on the clothesline. The conflicts between my brother, who had gotten into drugs and alcohol, and my father, who had his own covert drinking problem, erupted regularly. The tension in our home upset my mother, though she tried to hide it from me. I was so moved by my mother's tears that day, I promised I would protect her from the things my dad and brother did that upset her—then and in the future. In that moment, I went from being a kid who was enough to be president to a kid who could never meet the task I'd set for myself. I realize today that I had signed up for much more than I could deliver and certainly more than a 10-year-old boy should.

I know now that I wasn't responsible for the behavior that upset my mother, and I didn't have the power to protect her from it. It was a lie that I believed and that placed my ability to feel as if I was enough out of reach.

The resucceed download challenges you to realize you are 100 percent enough already, and you don't have to earn your way into an exclusive club of people who meet the admission requirements. Let me tell you how it works for me now: Being enough is a decision and internal belief. Simply put, the Creator of the Universe is enough, therefore we are too. We are enough because the Creator of the Universe has and is all that we need to be enough despite our humanity, fragility, shortcomings, and poor decisions. Believing this unlocks and supercharges our ability to fully show up in life without feeling like we have to earn our enoughness first.

When people look for validation of their *enoughness* outside themselves, they get tripped up. They listen for the right words from others and notice the right actions or results to show they've arrived. But you can't trust that what someone says or does has anything to do with you. Looking outside yourself for evidence of worth will always yield mixed results. You need to let that go and hold the belief that what you seek is already present. You are enough—simply enough.

What lie have you accepted that makes you not enough? Did you or someone else tell you or imply that you are not enough? It's important because your perceived lack in this area will drive you to pursue things that pull you away from your purpose and to create a mirage of enoughness instead. Investigating the moment when you decided you were not enough is the best thing you can do to interrupt the lie. I challenge you to go back to that moment. I'm here to tell you that it won't be hard to find. I was amazed at how quickly I arrived at my enoughness deficit moment once I sought it.

LIE #3: I can't connect the dots.

So much of the time, people try to connect the dots in their lives—meaning they draw significance from their skills, abilities, successes, and things in their past—to determine the direction or legitimacy of their future success. Resucceeding requires abandoning what you think you know because it's in the *not knowing* of your life that you grow the most and can truly resucceed.

Being comfortable with not knowing, rather than fabricating an answer off the top of your head, is vital to the resucceed system. The 5-Minute Epic Evening Ritual focuses on asking great questions and waiting for the answers to come instead of possessing great answers.

When we are young, we willingly take the leap from what we know to what we don't. So much of life is new and unknown at that time that we can't help doing this. When we become successful and celebrated for our success, we no longer want to risk the leap—and for the record, I'm not talking about the calculated risks you take in your career.

Doing something you desire or that you feel called to do seems like a bad choice if you're required to stick your neck out a little (or a lot) into the unknown. You want to stay with what has worked in the past, ask the questions you already have the answers for, and follow the path of least resistance.

That way of operating doesn't work for resucceeding. The biggest roadblock for already-successful, highly achieved individuals is they think they have all the answers. It isn't until they surrender to not knowing that the answers to the great questions we ask will come.

Here's an example: Let's assume you are a successful trial lawyer with a deep desire to use your skills and abilities to fight slavery in the developing world. You feel called to do this, but you limit yourself to your current range of skills and abilities. You know how to work and behave as a lawyer, and perhaps applying what you know would allow you to join your achievement with a high level of fulfillment and purpose.

It makes practical sense to join the path of fulfillment to your current path of success, so you seek to draw a line between the two. The lie here is believing that everything must line up and make logical sense. Your path to fighting slavery and finding fulfillment might lie elsewhere, but you can't find that out if you aren't open to a different answer to your question: How can I best help the victims of slavery in the world?

Connecting the dots is the worst thing you could do because you will invariably come up short. In fact, your mind will look for a reason to avoid resucceeding and stay in the miserable comfort of your current success.

I challenge you to set aside the need to connect the dots and have all the answers so you can make room for creative solutions that come from your subconscious mind and the miraculous. When we were born, we couldn't connect the dots. Still, we didn't have to remember to breathe or cry when we needed something. It simply happened. I am here to tell you that amazing things are happening all around us and that you absolutely do not have to rely on what you know to get where you are going anymore. The miraculous nature of life is open for business, and you are hired.

LIE #4: What we think is supreme.

We give our thoughts too much credit for diagnosing our situation and ascribing intent. In fact, what we think is often dead wrong—we don't figure it out until we're further down the road. Thinking can be our worst enemy when it comes to resucceeding.

A good friend of mine went hiking in a remote area alone and became lost without food, water, or direction. He thought he knew how to get out of the forest, but he learned that it wasn't until he surrendered and lifted up the question, that the answer arrived. By not knowing an answer, he received *the* answer, and about 24 hours after he'd gotten lost, he found his way back. Strange, isn't it? When he returned, he wrote a post on Facebook that resonated with me and speaks directly to this lie:

The most dangerous person in the world is the person who knows. I spent a very cold night on Mount Whitney because I knew. I knew I was right. Three different times I slammed a round peg in a square hole. Three times. Finally, on the fourth time, I decided maybe I didn't know, and I got God involved. I climbed toward the area I knew was not right. It was right. I had looked at that area so many times and did not even consider it. Not even a single thought because I knew I was right.

Your thoughts aren't always right. And you are not the only supreme thinker in your life. You won't be held back from resucceeding as you surrender to something bigger than yourself—whether you call that God, the miraculous, or presence. Rather, it is the start of your wonderful journey. The real challenge is that, most of the time, already-successful, highly achieved individuals think we have all the answers, but we don't. There is a profound power in acknowledging that you don't know and then waiting expectantly. Through the subconscious and miraculous, your answers will appear one by one.

Consider yourself fortunate right now. Knowing the destructive nature of these lies and how they interrupt your chance of resucceeding is 80 percent of the battle because you can spot the thoughts and talk back to them. It won't come naturally to you at first, but soon you will stop the lies and the actions that flow from them. In doing so, you pave the road to resucceed. Do yourself a favor and decide right now that these lies are no longer welcome in your life.

QUICK TAKEAWAY

In what areas of your life do you believe you are not enough? Not sure? Consider where you tend to overcompensate. That is the precise area where you feel you are not enough. Are you willing to get disgusted with your use of this lie that keeps you from resucceeding?

Are you ready to learn the resucceed system and the 5-Minute Epic Evening Ritual to use the hours when you sleep to transform your life? Or maybe you're thinking this whole thing is hocus pocus stuff that surely couldn't work, but you've read too far to stop now? Before you turn the page, consider this: You've taken advantage of your sleep in the past if you've ever "slept on" or "lifted up" a big decision or a problem when you weren't sure how to proceed. The resucceed system takes this casual practice and puts it on steroids, and in the next chapter, I will lay out how to do this.

Download complete yet? Once it is, I can't wait to unveil the 5-Minute Epic Evening Ritual. This is easy to do, and it takes just five minutes right before you go to bed. But first, I want to tell you about the power of sleep.

CHAPTER 6

THE 5-MINUTE EPIC EVENING RITUAL

The quality of your life is based partly upon the quality of the questions you ask yourself daily. If you are not inspired about your life or if you are not living the life you truly dream of, it just may be because you are not asking yourself the highest quality questions. The moment you do is the moment your life begins to change.

—JOHN F. DEMARTINI

Before I created the 5-Minute Epic Evening Ritual, I would make it to bed at about midnight (often after falling asleep in front of the television), and spend three to five minutes recording on a legal pad what I already knew I needed to do the next day. I also reviewed my master to-do list to see if I could include a few of those items as well. I planned how I would tackle my day and made sure I didn't forget anything.

After all that, I would attempt to have restful sleep. There was nothing life-affirming about this process. It created more stress in my waking life and while I slept. Adding stress right before bedtime is not a smart thing to do.

I'm sure I wasn't alone in staying up late. For many people, bedtime (and thus sleep) is expendable in our over-packed lives because waking up to get on with the day is not. This is especially true for highly achieved individuals. As we become more and more successful, we often get busier. We carve out slices of the time we need to recharge to add other activities we think are more important. But sacrificing sleep is a mistake.

Skipping sleep affects your memory, judgment, and performance. The Division of Sleep Medicine at Harvard Medical School collects and reviews studies on the effects of sleep deprivation on performance. Multiple studies show that the negative effects of sleep deprivation occur whether you pull an all-nighter or regularly miss an hour or two of the sleep your body needs.

Sleep is your reset button. It allows you to regroup, restore, and re-visualize the life you experience with a different lens, your internal lens, the one behind your eyes. Sleep is vital to an optimal life. It makes sense to make the most of your hours of slumber and be intentional about how you go about it.

Where does this urge to stay up late come from? As children, we dreamed of staying up late—like the grown-ups. We knew that something magical was happening after bedtime and hated the thought of missing out. I wonder if we hold on to the belief that something magical happens at night. It seems as if the older we get, the later we think we should stay up.

We have fallen for the myth that adults (again, especially successful ones) should not and cannot go to bed early. We have work to do, and if not, we've earned the right to reward ourselves and decompress after a challenging day. In doing so, I argue, we miss the real magic: a bedtime ritual that helps you ramp down for quality sleep that works for you and can change your life for the better. The 5-Minute Epic Evening Ritual is simple, and it starts with great questions you are willing to ask. Let me show you how I stumbled on this process.

THE OLD TO-DO LIST RE-ENVISIONED

For years, I kept a huge to-do list. I added everything from personal and household items to the nearly impossible to complete. The list was usually 80 items long, and I never completed all the items. Sound familiar? I noticed that I had a habit of completing only the easiest or most interesting things on the list. I wouldn't chip away at the hard but important items until they became urgent. The only reason I had such a long to-do list was because I worried I might forget some of the items. In a way, my to-do list became a *to-remember* list.

One evening several years ago, I approached my bedside table, and my yellow pad had gone missing. Instead I found that one of my kids had left some of the blank 3x5 cards they use for flashcards on my nightstand. It was late, and I decided to make do with what I had in front of me.

As I looked at the card, I thought, *wouldn't it be cool if my tasks for tomorrow would fit on the front of a 3x5 card?* That's when I realized I had gone about this whole bedtime-planning-for-the-next-day routine wrong. Instead of asking great questions about why I did things the way I did, who I am in my life, and how I showed up, I had been telling myself what to do, like a bad boss ignoring the signs of my ineffectual leadership.

I remembered that great bosses ask great questions. Not in condescending, pointed ways, but asking great questions with curiosity and learning from those that work for them. There is something profound that happens when successful people recognize that they don't know all the answers. I wondered what might happen if I asked myself great questions. That's how the 5-Minute Epic Evening Ritual was born. What I learned is that asking great questions right before you go to bed gives you access to one of the most undervalued resources in our lives: our sleep!

GREAT QUESTIONS

Each night as I arrive at my bedside, I view the stack of 3x5 cards as a chance to discover amazing truths I don't yet know. It's a magical time when I surrender to not knowing all the answers. Before I adopted the 5-Minute Epic Evening Ritual, I believed that, as a successful person, if I did not know the answer, I needed to go find it. Today, I choose to be vulnerable to the questions I don't know how to answer. Each night, I ask three types of questions, and then I go to sleep and let my subconscious through the creative and miraculous do the rest.

Once this became a practice for me, I ordered some extra thick, unlined 3x5 cards. I chose unlined because lines look like the start of a list, and I wanted to leave unrestricted room for creativity. Extra thick because the questions I would write would be substantial, so I felt the cards should be too. Also, I planned to take these cards with me the next day. The sturdier card stayed intact, even after being in my back pocket most of the day.

I loaded my pile of clean, substantial unlined 3x5 cards into my nightstand drawer with a single pen. Each evening, after tucking in my kids, turning off the lights downstairs, and brushing my teeth, I kneel next to my nightstand and write three resucceed questions.

These questions are not a mechanical reframe of directives and tasks into queries, but tough questions about things I don't yet know the answer to. Once asked, I wait expectantly to receive the answer.

There are three types of questions I ask myself each night: re-assess (where am I), re-engaging (what's most important), and re-affirming (core values). The rest of this book is about the questions, why they're important, and how to craft them using language to truly resucceed. I offer sample questions and explain the context for each to get you started. I encourage you to experiment: ultimately you will determine your nightly questions, and they may vary each night. However, I recommend that you try the question types in the order I've shared first. As I developed the 5-Minute Epic Evening Ritual, I noticed that the order affected my results. I sometimes glossed over the re-assess question or skipped it because I wasn't in the mood to evaluate after crafting the lighter, exploratory inquiries of the re-affirm and re-engage questions. The re-assess question of the 5-Minute Epic Evening Ritual forms the foundation for the other two resucceed questions, so I ask this question first each evening at bedtime. You don't need to worry about getting it wrong. By asking the three *Re-* questions right before you sleep, you can't help but resucceed.

THE RITUAL

The 5-Minute Epic Evening Ritual is like a bedtime prayer said in the form of three great questions. It is an invitation to open yourself to what you don't yet know about your life, your career, your future, and your purpose, along with what moves and shapes you. Through this practice, you too can experience the meaning, fulfillment, and joy you not only desire, but also deserve.

You deserve moments in life for introspection and clarity. You can gain this through the process of admitting you don't have all the answers and recording fundamental questions while trusting you will receive creative and miraculous answers while you sleep.

When you ask yourself great questions that are intentionally ordered and designed and write those questions down, you tap directly into your creative mind through the subconscious and access the miraculous while you sleep. And the results are amazing.

When I'm done writing my three great questions, I lay the card on top of my phone, which serves as my alarm clock. I keep it parked across the room on mute without vibration to avoid the temptation of looking at it one more time before I go to sleep or, even worse, hitting the snooze button in the morning, which would make me miss my Miracle Morning.

When I wake up, I read the questions as part of my Miracle Morning and wait expectantly for the answers. I carry the card with me all day as a physical reminder of holding the question in my mind. At the right time, the answers are revealed. These are the basics of the resucceed system.

QUICK TAKEAWAY

Have you ever gone to sleep thinking about a dilemma
and found that, when you awoke, you had the answer?
How did you think that happened? Was it like magic? You
probably didn't do it on purpose, but even if you did, you
weren't required to do anything more than think about the
problem (most likely in the form of a question). You went to
sleep not knowing and woke up with clarity. By asking the
great question about your current dilemma, you used the
power of your sleep to access your creative mind and the
miraculous for answers. The lessons are you didn't have
to make it happen and you didn't need to know anything
about the answer when you started.

I knew the 5-Minute Epic Evening Ritual worked, but I
needed to understand why. I imagine that you want to know
this too. In the next chapter, I explain that and the power
of sleep.

SPECIAL **FREE** BONUSES

5-MINUTE EPIC EVENING RITUAL

A Handy Reference for Those
Committed to Resucceeding

To download a comprehensive PDF of the entire 5-Minute Epic Evening Ritual, including sample questions, bedtime "ramp down" success routines, and tips and tricks, simply go to www.jamescolburn.net/resources.

FREE FAST LAUNCH PACKAGE

Give the Gift of Resucceeding

Many readers find the Resucceed system and the 5-Minute Epic Evening Ritual such a transformational process that they want to share it with those they love and care for. To help you help them, I have created what I call the "Free Fast Launch Package," which you can obtain by visiting www.jamescolburn.net/resources. By selecting the "Free Fast Launch Package," you can send your friends and loved ones the following for FREE:

- Three chapters of *Resucceed: Create an Extraordinary Future While You Sleep by Using the 5-Minute Epic Evening Ritual*

- FREE 5-Minute Epic Evening Ritual PDF Checklist

- FREE Training Videos and Audio on how to implement and immediately begin to Resucceed

I coach successful people to Resucceed. This is the answer to the call of my life. Each of us are called to fully "show up" in life with our unique brand and platform. My role in this is to help you bring forward hidden opportunities while exposing self-imposed limitations that hold you back. Seeing that light go on is my purpose. So much so, my logo is a light bulb.

All my coaching is done over the phone. This is by design to remove the typical obstacles to understanding. In most cases, you will never meet with me in person, which allows for a more meaningful, transparent coaching experience. Both coach and client find this helpful in the sharing and vulnerability that is necessary to resucceed.

I coach only highly successful, already-achieved individuals who seek to resucceed by adding fulfillment, meaning, passion, joy, and purpose to their lives.

Hire me when you seek one or more of the following:

- Emphatic desire to significantly increase your personal income

- Success that goes beyond what you have accepted and tolerated in your current brand of success

- Unquenchable interest in the 5-minute **Epic Evening Ritual** and how it can transform your life

- Profound new entrepreneurial startup that requires a new mindset and approach

- Energy management to get the most out of your work and play

- Clarification of purpose and strengths, and from this understanding, movement to the next level of success

My coaching clients have little to no patience for a long, drawn-out process, so my coaching agreements are never for longer than six months or more often than three times per month. My coaching clients come to me when they are absolutely ready to resucceed.

> **If you'd like to set up a personal 15 minute phone call with me, simply go to www.jamescolburn.net/coaching and follow the prompt to "Schedule a FREE 15-Minute Call." From there you will be directed to my scheduling application.**

CHAPTER 7

THE SCIENCE AND POWER OF PRODUCTIVE SLEEP

To achieve the impossible dream, try going to sleep.

—JOAN KLEMPNER

The 5-Minute Epic Evening Ritual works for the same reason that we sometimes "sleep on" a big or troubling decision. While we sleep, our mind works on the problem, rehearsing potential solutions in our dreams. The resucceed system is like supercharging your "sleep on it" muscle through daily practice and asking great questions. Most people use this mechanism from time to time, but those who employ the

5-Minute Epic Evening Ritual daily engage the creative mind seven days a week. We improve our ability to ask great questions and receive the answers.

Even if you have experience with sleeping on a difficult problem, you may wonder what it is that makes our sleep so powerful. Scientists have found out, and it provides support for the resucceed system.

EXTRINSIC AND INTRINSIC PATTERNING

Among the brain's many complex systems are the explicit pattern recognition system (or external) and implicit pattern recognition system (or internal). While awake, our brains rely on the explicit pattern recognition system, which means we use logic and rules to form our reality and take next steps. When we sleep, however, we use our implicit system, which relies on our intuition, skills, and experience.

Steven Kotler, the co-founder of the Flow Genome Project, described how "sleeping on it" works in a *Psychology Today* article. "When the explicit system is involved, the neurons that are talking to one another are usually found in close proximity. When the implicit system is at work, far flung corners of the brain are chit-chatting. Creativity … depends on those broader implicit networks putting together information in new ways." He said, "The secret, if there is one, is just about being able to relax enough for the intrinsic system to do its stuff."

By asking great questions right before we go to sleep, we jump-start our implicit system to connect the thoughts, notions, instincts, and facts across the mind. Ultimately, our great questions become the main work of our minds while we sleep, and it all starts with the great questions asked.

QUALITY SLEEP

To resucceed, you must create the opportunity for Rapid Eye Movement (REM) sleep. REM sleep is the phase when we dream, organize memories, and retain learning. Even a moderate shortage of REM can lead to changes in emotions, including our ability to regulate addictive impulses or avoid depressive thinking. REM sleep happens about 25 percent of the night and provides energy for the brain and body. It also supports your energy and overall mental and physical performance during the day. The resucceed system relies on REM sleep because this is where the miraculous effects of intrinsic patterning happen. You need plenty of REM sleep to make the most of your nighttime slumber.

Chances are you've heard about the importance of REM sleep, but you may not be familiar with its counterpart, Non-Rapid Eye Movement (NREM) sleep. NREM comprises the other 75 percent of our sleep. I like to describe it as the unconscious process of winding down from the day. During NREM sleep, we go through three different stages that take us from being awake to disengaging from our surroundings and allowing our bodies to relax. NREM sleep is necessary because it prepares the body for REM sleep, and because REM is so important to the resucceed system, you need to understand how to maximize your NREM sleep.

There are plenty of surefire ways to interrupt NREM, including eating late in the evening, drinking too much alcohol too close to bedtime, and screen time after dinner. You can probably identify the habits you engage in that interrupt your opportunity for restful sleep and REM because they are usually what you do too late and too often.

I looked for habits that interfered with my sleep and realized that having a drink at the end of the day became several drinks. Whenever I uncorked a bottle of wine in the evening, I committed to finishing the entire bottle. After all, I told myself, day-old wine never tastes the same. When I committed fully to the resucceed bedtime routine, I had to abandon the end-of-day drink because I rarely kept it to one, and I knew it interrupted my restful sleep. To stop this habit, I asked myself why I wanted the drink. When I didn't have a good enough answer, the choice became clear.

NREM is the unconscious ramping down that happens after you've laid your head on the pillow and begun to drift off to sleep. By turning off stimuli and eating earlier in the evening, along with drinking less alcohol or at least stopping long before bed, you set yourself up for a better night's sleep. And to be clear, a restful sleep means that you fall asleep quickly after you lie down to go to bed. Your ramp down process will ensure this. When you maximize your NREM sleep, you set yourself up for the REM sleep you need to resucceed.

Like all of us, you want to live the life of your dreams. This sentiment is so prevalent it's a cliché. Starting today, I'm taking the cliché out of "living the life of your dreams" because with the resucceed system and the 5-Minute Epic Evening Ritual, you can. Sleep will support every aspect of your life and fuel the pursuit of meaning and fulfillment.

The resucceed bedtime ritual is a permanent lifestyle change. But if you're worried about a constant struggle or that the ritual will feel like eating vegetables because they're good for you rather than for the enjoyment, fear not. Once you do it and see the results of resucceeding, your life will never be the same. As you engage the system, you will view your evenings not as an opportunity to burn the candle at both ends, but a time to focus on activities that create sanctuary and respite, a true opportunity to nurture and develop yourself. Once you develop the habit, you'll find that if you don't give this to yourself, you will miss it. Just like a proactive morning ritual, your evening ritual will become part of who you are.

QUICK TAKEAWAY

Is there something in your evening schedule or routine that you feel will get in the way of the 5-Minute Epic Evening Ritual? For me it was falling asleep in front of the television. I found that if I fell asleep downstairs, I wasn't alert enough for my 5-Minute Epic Evening Ritual. So, I had to do away with falling asleep downstairs, which meant that I need to go upstairs before I'm ready for sleep.

Take a minute to decide what you will need to change in your evening schedule or routine to give yourself the five minutes to write your three great questions and have restful sleep. You are worth this change.

Now that you understand how the ritual works, are you ready to learn about the three types of 5-Minute Epic Evening Ritual questions? In the next section, I begin by telling you about the re-assess question, which will help you evaluate whether certain aspects of your life are serving your highest good. If you are ready to resucceed and if you are interested in trying out the 5-Minute Epic Evening Ritual, then it's time to turn the page.

SECTION II

Re-Assess

What gets measured gets improved.

—PETER DRUCKER

To assess is to test, to appraise, to judge. At the heart of re-assessing is the intent to evaluate your life and work, form and function. Imagine these questions as the *getting real* part of the resucceed system. I encourage you to ask tough questions to take stock of your life and wait for honest answers in return. These questions will be the "you are here" marker on your journey seeking purpose and fulfillment.

Every day, you'll assess the current state of your life, and the possibilities vary from broad to specific: the focus of your business or how to tweak your diet for maximum energy. In this section, you'll find five short chapters that describe the components and context for your re-assess questions.

This area of inquiry seems to be the heaviest of the three. We'd rather focus on where we're going than aspects of the present circumstances we've become disgusted with. I encourage you to hold this lightly. Remember that you no longer need to have all the answers. Your job here is to ask great questions and stay open for the answers. Trust the creative and miraculous to provide the answers you don't yet know. This assessment becomes a journey of introspection. In my experience, what arrives is concise information about where you are, where you are going, and what you are working on. And it all happens while you sleep.

In the chapters ahead, you'll learn about the power of language, managing your energy, the limits of your comfort zones, resistance, and Lego time.

CHAPTER 8

LANGUAGE

*But if thought corrupts language, language can
also corrupt thought.*

—GEORGE ORWELL

The old saying "sticks and stones may break my bones, but words will never hurt me" rings in my ear as I write this chapter. The reality is that words can and do hurt you, especially the words you say to yourself. They have the power to keep you in survival success mode if you aren't careful. To resucceed in any area of your life, you must observe the way you speak to yourself about that area.

I'll repeat that: You must observe the way you speak to yourself.

As a practical matter, becoming the observer means you continue to speak to yourself as you always have. But the key difference is that you'll be looking for the power your language has over you. The good and the bad, how it limits you, and how you give words permission to own you.

Although evaluating your language is a re-assessing question, it is also an essential part of the entire resucceed system, so I have placed this question first. If you don't know how to ask excellent questions with great language during your 5-Minute Epic Evening Ritual, then resucceeding will be another obstacle and another way to self-sabotage.

The late Dr. Maxwell Maltz, an accomplished cosmetic surgeon and acclaimed author of the original *Psycho-Cybernetics*, was in a unique position to notice the impact that self-talk had on his patients' self-image. The ultimate success of the work he performed depended on not only his skills, but also how the patients viewed and spoke to themselves. He recommended that we "see ourselves with caring eyes." Be assured this has little to do with looking in a mirror. Instead, it's about the language we speak to ourselves every day. This reflects how we see ourselves.

If you view yourself with critical and judgmental eyes, then you aren't seeing the whole picture. I don't mean you should adopt a skewed version of your life that inflates or deflates the truth. Instead, strive for clear and honest observations when evaluating your life. Let your intention be for your highest good and becoming your best self. That requires caring eyes. Let me give you an example.

I have several personal rules I live by. These rules consist of habits that I've determined serve me beyond a shadow of a doubt. One of my rules is to start my day with a high level of gratitude. My feet can't hit the carpet until I feel a deep sense of gratitude. This was challenging at first, but over time I learned that starting my day in the right frame of mind was an incredibly powerful way to resucceed. The rule keeps my morning focused and forces me to play by a set of success game rules. Another important rule is getting up when my alarm goes off.

One morning, I hit the snooze button five times. Because my alarm is on the other side of the room from where I sleep, I got out of bed five separate times, walked five paces across the room to hit snooze, and walked five paces back to my bed to return to sleep. That's 50 steps before I was willing to start my day. I allowed my feet to hit the carpet before cultivating the feeling of gratitude.

When I finally got out of bed, it wasn't because I felt grateful for the opportunity to wake up. I was about to be late for my first meeting of the day: my workout. I broke more personal rules there.

When I arrived at the gym, I noticed I'd left my water bottle at home. After my shower, I realized I'd forgotten my dress shoes, and my tennis shoes did not go well with my suit. When I got in the car after my workout, I discovered I was almost out of gas (both for the car and my body, come to think of it). The list of things that had gone badly continued to grow. On more than one occasion during the day, I cursed myself out loud in the car for all that was going wrong and all the rules I had broken. Let's just say, if someone called me the words I had called myself, I'd no longer be their friend.

At my office, I tried to get through my email and collect myself when it dawned on me that I was kicking my own backend. I thought, *Hey, I'm supposed to be my own champion, right? Instead I'm being my worst enemy.*

It was in this moment, that I realized the power of assessing the way I speak to myself. By changing the way I spoke to myself and asking questions about how I could better thrive, even on those days when I felt off or when things didn't go according to plan, I started to resucceed in the area of language.

For example, I realized that if I call it a bad day, then it was a bad day. If I said something was hard, then it was hard. And if I decided a certain situation was like a punch in the gut, then it certainly felt that way. The trick was to realize and accept the power my language had over me and to start using language that didn't feel so bad. Once you can see it and you ask great questions about how you can treat yourself differently, insights will come.

Since language holds such power over us, I want you to see the language you use that holds you back from resucceeding. Fair warning: Don't read this if you aren't interested in changing your internal dialogue. Once exposed, your internal dialogue will never be the same.

1. YOUR INTERNAL LANGUAGE MUST BE CARING.

It's tempting to try to motivate yourself with a question like this: "What will it take to get me off my butt to do what I need to do?" Sure, this might work from time to time, but over the long haul you'll start to resent, perhaps even rebel against, the butt-kicking language you speak to yourself. The resucceed system is all about asking yourself great questions. Be curious about your internal dialogue. As you craft caring questions with love and respect right before you go to bed, you are much more prepared to receive great answers.

2. YOUR INTERNAL LANGUAGE MUST BE SPECIFIC.

It's common to ask vague questions about our life, but these rarely yield helpful answers. For example, compare these two questions: "Why don't I like to work out?" and "What would it take to spend one hour managing my energy at the gym so I can resucceed?" The second question challenges you in a caring and respectful way with a specific timeline and reminds you why you want to work out. Energy doesn't sound like toil, sweat, agony, and guilt with a shower. It sounds like a cool thing we'd be thrilled to add to our day. The first question assumes you don't like to work out and implies that something is wrong with you; it's the equivalent of a slap in the face. A part of you might be curious about the answer to this question, but in truth, it's rhetorical and designed to evoke shame.

Remember, your goal is to ask a question because you *don't* know the answer but are open to receiving insight. Even if you suspect you know *an* answer, by asking a great question, you will arrive at one that is often better. Chances are you don't know why you don't do what you know you should be doing. You only know that you *don't do it* and that you *should be doing it*. You're probably sick of adding *should-dos* to your to-do list because it adds responsibility without a clear return. It becomes something you rebel against. You know all this, *and* you are ready to discover how you can start managing your energy on a regular basis. That's when the magic happens.

3. YOUR LANGUAGE MUST BE SIMPLE.

Although your questions should be specific, they should not be complex. You're asking these questions right before sleep, and this process is designed to take five minutes. This is not a time for fancy words and phrases. Aim for succinct and inquisitive questions that tap directly into your creative mind and the miraculous for the answers you don't yet know. For example, "What's one area of my life that deserves reflection while I am working out tomorrow?" instead of "How can I use self-reflective techniques to uncover some of my most glaring areas of dysfunction while I am at the gym tomorrow morning?"

4. YOUR LANGUAGE MUST BE ACTION ORIENTED.

Your questions must prompt action. Great thoughts are helpful, but great action makes things happen in your life. You ask because you want an answer that will provoke an active response.

A good example of this is the core question I used to write this book. For the longest time, I hoped for a big block of downtime, a marathon session of complete peace and blissful writing. I thought about authors I'd seen depicted in movies: writing while looking at a picturesque seascape or winter scene. No whining kids, competing activities, or chores.

My initial question was, when can I find the adequate downtime to finish my book? One day I realized that I have three kids, a crazy life, loads of responsibilities, and two full-time jobs. (I'm not complaining; I like it this way. In fact, I get more done when I'm busy.) Given these circumstances, why was I hoping for endless downtime to write a book? I changed the question right then: How can I find daily inspiration in my crazy life that is so compelling I must sit down and write another chapter in the book, even if I think I don't have time? The key words here are *daily, must, write,* and *another chapter.*

QUESTIONS

You can use these questions to get started, adapt them to match your circumstances, or craft your own to re-assess how you speak to yourself.

1. What would it look like to speak to myself with love, even when I'm attempting to challenge my behavior or feeling frustrated with myself?

2. What words or phrases move me to take immediate action?

3. What words and phrases do I speak to myself that shut me off from resucceeding?

4. Would it be possible to speak more words of encouragement than disfavor when I wake up?

5. What language do I use that tears me down and keeps me from resucceeding?

Let's be honest. You are the person who controls the language you speak to yourself. No one else is in charge of that. Sure, the way people spoke to you as a child influenced how you talk to yourself. But it's important that you observe and choose today. Only you can properly re-assess that language because no one else can hear your internal dialogue. To re-assess your language then refine and adjust it is to resucceed. As you change your language, your life will change too.

QUICK TAKEAWAY

Stop the next time you do something that upsets you and listen to your internal dialogue. I like to imagine that I'm watching myself from above. It helps me take on the role of a dispassionate observer. Whether it's as simple as saying something that didn't come out right or as complex as not nailing your business presentation, listen to the words you say to yourself. Do you sound irritated, or do you build yourself up with language that is caring, actionable, and specific? Review the language guidelines above (make your language caring, specific, simple, action oriented, and measureable) and immediately craft a resucceed question that challenges you to be your best without using words that tear you down.

Observing and changing the way you speak to yourself and resucceeding in general requires massive energy to break the gravitational pull of old patterns and beliefs. Learning what fills you up and what drains you is an essential part of this process. In the next chapter, I tell you what I noticed one day at the gym that forever changed the way I manage my energy.

CHAPTER 9

MANAGING YOUR ENERGY

*Physical fitness is not only one of the most important
keys to a healthy body, it is the basis of dynamic
and creative intellectual activity.*

—JOHN F. KENNEDY

Without expansive energy, we don't have the stamina and vitality to resucceed. Energy starts with energy management (what most people call exercise) and nutrition. But this is not a chapter to help you adopt a great diet and exercise plan. Instead, I urge you to ask great questions about the diet and exercise plan you need to have massive energy. The goal is to have the energy necessary to resucceed today, tomorrow, and as we grow older.

When it comes to energy management, I contend that we've gone about it all wrong. Most people view the drive to the gym as a dutiful chore they want to rebel against, not a bountiful opportunity. When they think about these activities, thoughts (or threats) of what will happen if they don't follow through come to mind. A "you-better-do-it-or-else" edict on your to-do list. Of course, their rebellious nature kicks into full gear.

Energy management can be enjoyable, and you no doubt love those endorphins, but if it's a do-or-die mandate, you're already on your way to failure. For purposes of resucceeding and the 5-Minute Epic Evening Ritual, we move energy management and nutrition from chore to transformational opportunity. I'm not talking about using willpower or suggestive positive chatter. The resucceed system changes your motivation for regular exercise and proper nutrition, and it starts with the excellent questions you ask yourself at bedtime—or other times.

One day at the gym, I was warming up on an elliptical machine that had a great view of people coming up the stairs. I noticed that almost everyone, young and old, dragged themselves up the stairs to start their cardio workout. Once they reached the top, many would compose themselves, take a drink of water, and find a machine, go to a spin class, or visit the aerobics studio.

While people worked out, they appeared to have good energy, but most struggled with the stairs. I couldn't get this out of my mind that day, and before bed, I asked myself an excellent energy management question: What type of exercise or activity would help me better manage my energy to resucceed? I didn't overthink it, just wrote it down and trusted the process.

The next morning, I approached the stairs and felt the urge to sprint up them two at a time as fast as I could. When I reached the top, I couldn't believe how great I felt.

"That's how," I heard in my head. I had just received the answer to my great question.

As I picked an elliptical machine, I asked a second energy management question: What is the exercise I do now that *takes away* my energy? I didn't even have to sleep on it. The answer came immediately: the elliptical machine. I realized that working out on one machine for 30–45 minutes, or doing any one thing in the gym for that length of time is a boring and mind-numbing activity. The key was to do the things that people struggle to do when they don't have energy. Think about what an older person can't do because they haven't managed their energy for 20 or 30 years. I did those things (bounding up the stairs, for example) in as many areas and as often as I could.

I offer several ideas here as a guide to help you do the things that people who lack energy can't or won't do. Keep in mind that I'm not a doctor, exercise physiologist, or nutritionist. (Before changing your diet or exercise regime, it's a good idea to check in with your doctor.) My expertise in this area comes from managing attitudes, thoughts, and beliefs. I understand that struggles with exercise and nutrition usually have more to do with mindset than discipline. When your mindset changes, your discipline will follow.

ENERGY MANAGEMENT

Movement

Run the stairs whenever you can. Do it 15–20 times per workout. Not just at the gym but with any stairway where it's appropriate.

Bursts

I found that six to ten minutes of full-out bursts on the treadmill or elliptical machine is 100 percent more effective than a 45-minute cardio drudge. Some people call this hit training. I call it resucceeding. Picking energy management activities that allow you to forget you are exercising is not the intent (so don't stay on the treadmill just because you haven't finished a show). Feel the exercise. Embrace the movement. Then go on with your day.

Jump

No surprise, people that don't have energy don't jump. So jump!

Bend and Stretch

Flexibility is reserved for the energetic. As we bend, we stretch (literally and figuratively, I've learned).

Strength Training

I don't see a lot of 80-year-olds at my gym doing strength training. In fact, what I see is a lot of 40-year-old men who look six to eight months pregnant, and they usually walk or run (sort of) on a treadmill for what seems like an eternity. In my experience, strength training burns more fat than cardio activities ever will. What is the biggest room in every gym? You guessed it, the one devoted to cardio. Why is this? I suspect it's because you can walk, run, glide, or do whatever you choose on a cardio machine without thinking about it too much. Strength training required focus, skill, structure, and intention. I challenge you to keep it simple, but add in some strength training.

Relax

It may seem counterintuitive to discuss relaxing along with energy management and proper nutrition, but it's important you understand this: those who don't manage their energy, don't relax. Relaxing in this context is similar to the recovery phase in exercise parlance. Relaxing while you work out is something people often forget. Try it! Relax your face, your shoulders, your arms, or whatever is tense while you exercise, and you will go faster, lift more, and run longer. In any area where you want to improve, relax.

Relaxing is a habit you must cultivate. The more you practice, the more you will relax on cue. When you're done working out, give yourself an opportunity to relax and center. Take a seat and get comfortable. Take some deep breaths. Appreciate the gift you have given yourself; blessed that you just managed your energy.

When I think about relaxing and the counterintuitive nature of this advice, I'm reminded of a story Darren Hardy, the former publisher of *Success Magazine*, once told. He said he had been in a spin class and toiling to increase his speed when the instructor asked him if he knew how to go faster. Hardy answered that he didn't. The instructor told him to relax, and that did the trick.

If you're a runner, then you know how this works. As you relax into your run, you enter flow and begin to glide. As you loosen your muscles, you go faster, not slower. Try this with any exercise, but also in any area of your life where you want to increase your speed. It works every time. Relaxing is a mind thing. Control the tension in your mind, and you become faster, stronger, and more powerful. This is resucceeding.

NUTRITION

Eat Clean, Alive Food

Choose food you must rinse before you eat because it comes directly from the earth. Another simple tip is to choose food that is colorful instead of white. Eat food with ingredients that you know. Processed food is not great for managing your energy. Personally, I use the Mediterranean Diet as a guide for good nutrition. This regimen doesn't even feel like a diet, so it makes long-term sustainability way more possible.

Moderation

You can love pizza but schedule it. Allow yourself to love pizza during your scheduled pizza enjoyment evening. Ours is Friday night. I wait all week for it.

Eat More Slowly

Take your time when you eat, and you will enjoy it more. Taste the food instead of getting it down as quick as you can for the next item on your fork. As you eat more slowly, you become full more quickly. Once you become full, you will stop eating, which means you will eat less and likely lose weight.

Drink Lots of Water

I drink at least one-third my weight in ounces of water per day. I weigh around 200 pounds, so that's about 66–70 ounces. I start my day with 20 ounces of high alkaline water as part of my Miracle Morning. We don't hydrate before or during sleep, so by the time you wake, your brain is desperate for water. It makes no sense to drench it in brown hot water (coffee) in the morning. Instead of, or at least in addition to, your coffee, drink cool (not freezing) water to start your day off right. Full disclosure: I drink one cup of coffee every morning. But, I go heavy on the water and light on the brown hot water. (By the way, call it brown hot water. When you change your language, you change the meaning and often your behavior.)

Energy Foods

Eat foods that you know provide energy. Watch for the foods that give you a boost. Notice the foods you eat that drain your energy. Do certain types of protein or carbs make you feel lazy or foggy? Does sugar put you to sleep? This is the antithesis of energy, so limit the foods that don't serve you.

QUESTIONS

With these tips and the following five great energy management questions, I trust that your energy will improve quickly. Focus on questions that get to the bottom of what it would take to change your energy management and nutrition habits to give you maximum energy—more energy than anyone else at your age—to resucceed.

1. What activity in my current energy management routine takes energy from me?

2. Why do I want to eat or drink certain foods that I know drains me or doesn't add to my energy level?

3. What high-energy activity would maximize my ability to resucceed?

4. What rules do I have in place that give me an excuse not to work out?

5. What small tweaks could I make to my diet to give me the edge in my looks, energy, and vitality?

QUICK TAKEAWAY

Tonight during your 5-Minute Epic Evening Ritual, ask yourself, "What is one thing I could do for energy management and nutrition to maximize my energy tomorrow?" Wait for the answer in the morning. Your energy controls how you feel and live. If you don't have energy, I guarantee you will struggle at resucceeding. Your energy does not necessarily come from working harder at the gym or skipping tacos during lunch. It comes from the great questions you're willing to ask yourself right before you go to bed and acting on the answers that arrive.

Now that you're on your way to managing your energy and eating well, I'd like to help you take a step out of your comfort zone. What if I told you that your comfort zone is keeping you from resucceeding? In the next chapter, I describe the various forms of comfort zones we cling to and how they keep us from what matters most to us.

CHAPTER 10

COMFORT ZONES

*For cool things to happen, you have to get out
of your comfort zone.*

—RONY ABOVITZ

We all have a comfort zone, the circumstances (people, places, and things) that feel safe, where we can relax. Most people dwell in their comfort zone. It's not stressful there, and they know what to expect. It might not be the best place, or even what they want, but at least it's *comfortable*.

Life often calls you to be courageous instead of comfortable. The first step is to re-assess and acknowledge your comfort zone and how you gravitate toward it. When you see it clearly, you take away its power and pull on you. As you rely on your comfort zone less and less, you become more.

While attending my oldest son's soccer games many years ago, I found myself making assumptions and creating stories about each parent on the sidelines. Inside my head, I decided what type of person each parent was. Whether caring, successful, annoying, addicted, or arrogant, I *knew* who the parents were before I had introduced myself to them.

It's hard to share this because I worry what you'll think of my being so judgmental and sure of my beliefs about people I didn't know. But I realize I'm not that different from most people when it comes to judging others by their appearance in one venue. In fact, I'm sure the same parents I evaluated had misjudged (or maybe correctly judged) me. This is what we do to avoid leaving our comfort zone.

One day, I spoke to one father who had attempted to talk with me before (despite the distance I'd kept from him). In the past, whenever he approached me, I would act as if I were interested in the game so he would get the hint. I soon felt bad about that and decided to get to know Paul.

To my amazement, Paul was the opposite of what I'd assumed. In fact, knowing him has been a huge blessing to my business and career. It started when I left my comfort zone and got to know him.

The thing to understand about your comfort zone is that it has more to do with insecurities than comfort. We use comfort zones to feel safe. Safe from failure, vulnerability, and insecurity. Instead of growing and stretching, we cling to our comfort zone to maintain the status quo. Yet, if we're honest, the status quo we seek is not possible in the long run. All that comfort will be gone one day.

Let me show you what I mean with another example. Back in my early real estate days, I met Larry and Joan, an older couple selling their first (and last in their case) home, where they had raised two children and lived for 50 years. When Joan experienced symptoms of dementia and Larry's health problems prevented him from keeping up with the house, they decided to move to a nearby assisted living facility.

When I visited them the first time, I realized that Larry and Joan had surrounded themselves with things that were important to them. They weren't hoarders, and their house was neat and tidy. Nonetheless, it was full of sentimental belongings. Even the yard contained keepsakes—mounds of rocks, each with a story, including an agate from the Oregon coast and geodes from Warsaw, Iowa.

They asked if I could help sell some of their big personal items that might remain as we neared the closing of the sale. As an eager real estate agent, I told them I would. Little did I know what I'd agreed to do.

When the closing date approached, I went to see what they had left at the house. I imagined some boxes and maybe a few larger items: rock cutting machines, a piano, and a huge chest of drawers that wouldn't fit in their assisted living apartment. It would be a quick visit, I assumed, long enough to take a few photos to put the items up for sale online.

When I arrived, I was shocked to see that, other than a few personal items and their clothes, the home looked fully furnished. Little had been moved or changed since my first visit. I felt confused because most of my elderly clients asked their adult children (or other relatives) to help them pack and move and to take the sentimental items off their hands. Larry and Joan had already moved, and I thought they would need or want some of the items that had surrounded them for 50 years.

With no other option or time remaining, I hired a moving company to take the important items to a storage unit, and I donated or threw away everything else. As a friend and I worked on emptying the house, I had plenty of time to think. I felt sad about the couple's letting their belongings go. In the same moment, I realized how much we hold on to stuff for decades that, in the end, means so little. Then, in a flash, we let it all go. Whether we make a move like Larry and Joan or simply pass away, we leave it all behind.

Your comfort zone, like the items in Larry and Joan's home, won't last forever, so you have no reason to, and will derive no benefit from, treating it as if it will. The better course, and the way to resucceed, is to change your relationship with the people, places, and things in your comfort zone.

Everyone's comfort zone looks different. What they have in common is that they keep you from authentic relationships with yourself and others. Like an adult version of a childhood blankie, people surround themselves with stuff, events, positive and negative attention, and even abusive relationships. This is because life within the comfort zone is far less intimidating and daunting than the unknown prospect and risks associated with abandoning them.

For Larry and Joan, it wasn't until circumstances forced them to move into a much smaller place that they let their comfort zone go. What had been so important quickly dissipated the moment they transitioned to a new life. Not that they didn't have mixed feelings about leaving everything behind, but when life required it, they let go.

This reality raises critical questions: What would it take for you to let go of your comfort zone right now? What would life look like for you? Is there perhaps a new life out there once you release your comfort zone to see it? I argue that you would resucceed.

SAMPLE QUESTIONS

The re-assessing comfort zone questions focus on those things, tangible or not, that you lean on and cling to and that keep you from meaning and fulfillment. As you open yourself to investigating the comfy blanket of your comfort zone, you open to the magic of the unknown that was right in front of you the entire time.

QUESTIONS

Here are a few great comfort zone questions to help you step into your stretch zone.

1. Who in my life have I mistakenly kept at arm's length—to stay in my comfort zone—that I should get to know immediately?

2. What is one tangible or intangible person, place, or thing that I cling to that will keep me from resucceeding tomorrow if I do nothing?

3. What in my life do I continue to surround myself with that, one day, I know will matter very little in the grand scheme of things?

4. What go-to feeling do I attempt to recreate as a comfort zone that keeps me from progress?

5. What conversation needs to happen that I've been avoiding to stay in my comfort zone?

QUICK TAKEAWAY

Imagine you called a real estate agent to sell the family home you've lived in for 50 years. You know that you will move to a space that is 75 percent smaller than your current home. Look around you. What are the few things that matter most to you that you will keep? Now, what would you leave behind that you always thought you'd keep near and dear? Is there value in letting go of those things today? Even if you aren't moving, letting these things go would help you resucceed in your life and open yourself to the fulfillment, meaning, and passion you have always sought.

Letting go is rarely easy, and resistance may be the hardest thing to release. In the next chapter, I explain how happy hour was perhaps the biggest reason I took so long to write this book. You'll learn how to uncover your own resistance so you can do what you have been designed to do in your life.

CHAPTER 11

RESISTANCE

*Resistance is a powerful motivator precisely because it
enables us to fulfill our longing to achieve our goals
while letting us boldly recognize and name the
obstacles to those achievements.*

—DERRICK A. BELL

I can't tell you how many times I went to happy hour or
the gym instead of writing a chapter in this book. Resistance
became a pivotal topic as I realized something huge: Although
I knew what I needed to do, I often did the opposite.

Interestingly enough, what we do to resist what we should do isn't always bad. It's just unproductive. For example, going to the gym and exercising is a positive activity, but going there instead of doing what I needed or had planned to do is a massive form of resistance. I hadn't realized this until I was called to write this book. I have experienced more resistance in my life while writing this book than during any other project I have attempted to date. What that tells me is that this book is a big deal. Why else would I resist it?

Here is another example to illustrate resistance to something I felt called to do. As part of my 5-Minute Epic Evening Ritual, I once asked, "God, what would be a good word or words that you would like to share with me?"

The question had been on my mind for a while, but I hadn't been ready to ask it in part because I was afraid of the answer. I finally opened myself to what I would hear. This is important because I've learned you can't ask resucceed questions if you can't receive the answers. You've got to be willing to accept what comes and at least be willing to consider responding to the answers.

The next morning, I woke at 5:00 a.m. for my Miracle Morning, made a pot of coffee, and sat down in the living room for some music, reflection, and gratitude. Once I finished my ritual, I said, "Okay, God, I'm open to that good word I asked for last night." Before I could finish the sentence, I heard loud and clear, "You need to stop drinking alcohol for a while."

That was not the answer I had been expecting. It seemed so trivial. How could this be God's good word for me?

I should note that drinking had been a social thing for me about 90 percent of the time. A reward for a productive week, celebrating or appreciating a friend, or a way to enjoy the finer things in life. The remaining 10 percent was an attempt to change my state. These were the rough days when I was frustrated or struggling with a decision, and I used alcohol to escape.

Over the next four weeks, I didn't change a thing but found myself confronted with a recurring challenge wherever I turned. First, I noticed great men and women who either didn't drink or drank only a little. People in books, those I met, and others I hadn't known didn't drink. It wasn't that they had never consumed alcohol, but they felt compelled to stop or modify their habits. They decided they had important things to accomplish, and drinking got in the way.

During that period, I continued to drink as usual. Happy hours with friends, dinner with my family, sometimes alone while enjoying a cigar on the back patio. Not too much or too often. Each time I drank, I felt less and less fulfilled by it. In fact, the beverages I often enjoyed started to taste more like a chemical, and that confused me.

One evening at a restaurant with friends, I ordered a steak, the kind that deserved a fine red wine pairing. When the waiter asked for my drink order, I didn't want wine or any other alcohol with dinner. I hadn't demonized it or thought it was bad or dangerous for me; it just didn't sound good. I ordered an Arnold Palmer (ice tea with lemonade) instead. My friends looked at me oddly. I shrugged my shoulders because I was confused too. Then we went on with dinner.

From that day, I haven't considered myself a drinker. I don't feel as if I quit drinking because I didn't. I've had a drink from time to time, but it's no longer on my radar. My relationship with drinking changed during that dinner. I'm not thirsty for it any more. Perhaps for a season or a lifetime (I didn't know at the time), the good word for me was not to drink, and I responded to it.

Not long after distancing myself from the regular consumption of alcohol, I realized how much I had leaned on the habit to feel comfortable in a social situation, the 90 percent I mentioned before. The opportunity allowed me to learn that I don't need to drink. I am naturally social, and I enjoy developing a rapport with people and finding common ground we can talk about.

Drinking seemed to hinder that process. By skipping it, I became more aware of my conversations and how I showed up in them. I also noticed that my choice made others feel a little uncomfortable. My friends seemed to think I was judging them for drinking. And I wasn't. In fact, I don't notice when others drink. It's just not on my radar anymore. I notice when others drink too much, but not out of judgment. I recognize that drinking is a form of resistance *in me*. By stopping for a time and limiting it thereafter, I could complete this book.

This habit had been an obstacle to answering the call my whole life, but especially while writing this book. I would intend to write a few chapters while enjoying a few drinks at a local restaurant or in my backyard. As I drank, I found that my mind wandered. The next thing I knew, I was surfing social media or reading my email. Soon, drinking became an excuse not to write.

Answering the call to share the resucceed system and the 5-Minute Epic Evening Ritual was a big challenge. I had to stretch way outside my comfort zone to do this. Drinking was the reason I didn't get as far as I'd hoped and why my words weren't as clear as I wanted them to be. I placed drinking between me and my ability to respond to the call of my life.

The re-assessing resistance questions represent a willingness to recognize the areas of your life where resistance impedes your pursuit of purpose here on earth. It's being open to asking, what habits hold me back from personal fulfillment? What could I stop doing today that would produce immediate results in responding to my life's call? Said another way, what do I allow to get between me and my highest and best self?

Resistance is tricky: It doesn't always manifest as a vice and can be subtle in our lives. Although it's a form of self-sabotage, that doesn't make it obvious. It can seem honorable or valiant. For example, when your current success keeps you from resucceeding. You could use marriage counseling to avoid working on your marriage. Or, you could use your busy work schedule to resist dealing with a family issue. Resistance lurks behind activities that seem positive on the surface and those that don't serve us.

Resistance is not a one-size-fits-all proposition. A single action performed by different people, or the same person at different times, could be progress or resistance. The form it takes and where it shows up in your life will be unique to you, though your version of it may have certain characteristics in common with others.

The following is a list of activities that *can be* manifestations of resistance. I encourage you to consider the list and add your own examples. You may notice that some of the items are opposites. As I mentioned, one person's positive act is another's resistance. Also, some activities don't constitute resistance when done in moderation. It might help to add "too much" to see if the activity is an area of resistance for you.

1. Drinking
2. Smoking
3. Surfing the Internet
4. Social media
5. Obsessively tracking your to-do list
6. Coaching or counseling appointments
7. Organizing and preparing
8. Reading new books
9. Cleaning
10. Exercising instead of working
11. Working instead of exercising
12. Pursuing perfection in any area of your life
13. Reliving past events in your mind (past successes, past failures, past anything)
14. Proofreading (a personal favorite)
15. Over attachment to our current success and accolades in fear of losing them
16. Busyness or performing insignificant tasks while ignoring what's most important
17. People pleasing
18. Thinking about something but not deciding or acting
19. Parsing words or holding your tongue in conversations
20. Putting everyone first and yourself last
21. Getting further education

22. Intellectualizing or overthinking to avoid making a wrong or hasty decision

23. Saving money

24. Spending money

25. Making excuses for yourself or others

26. Not forgiving yourself or others

27. Taking medications

28. Using pride to keep others at arm's length or help you feel significant

29. Lack of confidence

30. Overconfidence

31. Risk taking

Reread the list from time to time and stay curious about what stands between you and your calling.

One last point about resistance: Understand that resistance is a multi-layered problem. Whenever you expose one area of resistance in your life and seek to understand it or remove it, other habits will arise. Exposing and responding to it is a game changer. If you have questions, know that the creative mind, through the subconscious and the miraculous, is the best judge of where you're resisting your call. This is one area where you can transform your life if you stay open and curious.

QUESTIONS

Here are five great re-assessing resistance questions to get you started. The goal is to expose the activities in your life, even if valiant and honorable, that you do instead of what you are called to do before you die. Yep, it's that big. So go big and deep with these questions:

1. What is one thing I do as a fall back when I am not feeling confident or capable of doing what I'm called to do?

2. God, if I decided I was willing to receive and respond to a few great words of wisdom tomorrow morning, what would they be?

3. What are the subtle things I do or think that keep me from showing up in [the resisted activity]?

4. In what area of my life do I use my confidence and assert my power to keep others away or isolate myself from growth opportunities?

5. In what areas of my life can I take what I've learned and integrate it rather than resist the information?

QUICK TAKEAWAY

What is the one activity you rarely make time to do that, when you finally get to it, you feel guilty that you don't do it more often?

Next, consider the activities in your life you use to resist doing the one thing you know you should be doing. Be honest. What's your grand excuse for not making the time? Your answer is most likely a go-to excuse to resist the thing you are called to do, the thing that is a core responsibility or purpose while you're here on earth.

Here's an example from my life, one that most parents can relate to. My resistance keeps me from spending alone time with my kids. Whenever I make the time, I feel bad that I don't do it more often. In the next chapter, you'll learn how Lego Time changed that for me.

I've worked to change this and now schedule special time with each of my kids. In the next chapter, you'll learn how my coach taught me that playing Legos with my kids would ultimately help me earn $300,000 more in income.

CHAPTER 12

LEGO TIME

Don't be in a hurry to achieve your dreams. Take a day to play with your kids and relax—your dreams will still be there tomorrow.

—LINDSEY RIETZSCH

L et me tell you about how playing Legos changed my life.

Years ago, after achieving great financial success, I knew I needed a personal tune-up. This was right about the time when I went on the epic Costco run to distract myself from my failure to achieve one more sale on Christmas Eve. That event catalyzed a period of personal reflection. I decided that, if I wanted to go to the next level, I must hire a coach to help me work on the areas of my life and work that were out of whack.

When our coaching relationship began, I told my coach that my main goal in working with her was to make $300,000 more this year than I had made the year prior. I was ignoring the core issue that had presented itself on Christmas Eve that I mentioned in chapter 2.

As I type this chapter, I can't help but realize how often we are rewarded for our incessant focus on all the wrong things. Although there was nothing wrong with my desire for coaching, I still didn't get that I was chasing the wrong dream. I knew I needed coaching, but I wasn't sure if I was willing to focus on something I couldn't monetize. I needed the expense to lead to bottom-line results. But my coach had other ideas. She could tell the difference between what I truly need and what I was using to quiet the call to my higher purpose.

After our first session, she asked one simple but transformational question: "Do you play Legos with your kids?"

This caught me off guard. What did this have to do with making another $300,000 in the next year? I worked out an answer to her question, but I was a stuttering mess. I told her I struggled to play with my kids because I couldn't take my mind off my work and other responsibilities. The truth? The rapid-fire thoughts that arose when I was messing around with the kids and playing Legos, instead of working, made my head feel as if it would explode.

My coach didn't respond. The silence was powerful for me because I replayed what I had just said. My answer made me look one-dimensional. I wondered how my business could become so all-consuming to make me feel justified in not playing with my kids. I knew then that this was a big moment in my coaching, and I was eager to learn more.

"James, I can't help you make $300,000 more," my coach finally said, "until you are willing and able to enjoy playing Legos with your kids."

As I write this, I feel goosebumps remembering the power of this statement. Preoccupation with my success kept me from playing with my kids, and I had no idea how to be okay with the new awareness. I also didn't know how to focus on something other than how to be more financially successful and monetize every moment of my life, but I knew I needed to learn.

It pains me to think about this. I missed so many moments of life with my kids because of my relentless pursuit of more achievement and success; I was missing meaning, fulfillment, purpose, and joy. The fact that I couldn't play with my kids was a huge problem, and I realized my coach was on point.

Her question reminded me that nothing in my business plan was designed to help me be compassionate and alive. I attended to the *what* of my working life rather than the *why*. Though the Costco trip was a red flag that something was wrong, I thought I could solve it with an additional $300,000 per year.

The point I had missed is that success without a deep relationship with my wife and children was empty, not to mention the need for a right relationship with myself, and I couldn't fill that empty feeling inside with more money. That is one thing I'd already proven. This focus on the chase to the exclusion of time with my family was a pernicious form of resistance. My goal had been to work for my family's comfort and security, but the way I was going about it wasn't working for any of us.

For the next year, my coach and I worked on what we named the "How to Be Compassionate and Alive" plan. The result was a clear list of core responsibilities that I knew I needed do before anything else:

1. Listen with my eyes, not just my ears. People know I'm listening by how I attend to them while they are talking.

2. Be interested in others.

3. Recognize other people's genuine strengths.

4. Act on my generosity.

5. Play Legos with my kids often.

This process allowed me to focus on my *why* instead of the next transaction I was working on. It helped me prioritize time with those I love most.

The plight of the highly successful individual is never more illuminated than when looking at their approach to and care for downtime. Downtime can be a poignant time of reflection, growth, and recharge or a source of stress, unease, and frustration.

In the blunt words of Stephen King, "Get busy living or get busy dying." There's no benefit in alienating everyone you love and care for as you chase a new and improved version of success. Success that requires alienating others eventually will leave you with an utter lack of meaning, fulfillment, and purpose. It is in your moments of downtime, when you're alone or with those you love, that you have the opportunity for expansive personal and evolved growth. And, it starts with a great question.

The 5-Minute Epic Evening Ritual is for every day of the week, including your days off, weekends, staycations, and vacations. If you take the time for this practice, you will experience some of the most rapid resucceed growth there is.

Here's how the re-assess Lego Time question goes for me. I approach home on Friday evening knowing the kids are waiting for me so we can go get pizza which has become a weekly Colburn tradition. Once we get home from dinner and tuck the kids in their beds, I make my way to my nightstand. Knowing I have the next two days off from my normal work routine, I ask the Lego Time re-assess question.

Lego Time for me is a metaphor for the person I seek to be during my downtime, and this question is about how I will give myself to others over the next two days, not just to my kids, but also my wife, friends, and other people I encounter. Like all the resucceed questions, this one must be actionable and thoughtful, but it also must set an intention for how I want to feel while I enjoy time with family and friends over the weekend.

Notice that I include friends. Lego Time isn't always focused on your immediate family. Once I asked, how can we make new friends by spending more time each month with people we really like but don't know that well? I envisioned people from our neighborhood we'd never gotten to know, the parents of our children's friends we pass in the hallways at school, and people from our church that we see in the lobby on Sundays.

The next morning, I awoke with the idea to hold a monthly dinner. The question was so powerful, and the answer seemed so easy and fun. Right away, I ordered 100 preprinted invitations with blanks so we could add the date of the dinner each month.

For months and months, Maurita and I invited special acquaintances to our home for dinner. It was fulfilling to connect in this way, and I even enjoyed seeing how shocked people were that we had no agenda other than a deeper friendship. I would wait until we were in the middle of dinner and then say something like this: "Well friends, the purpose of our meeting here is ... Amway." Then the room would erupt in laughter because people expect there to be an agenda, and there wasn't one.

I can tell you having new friends over for dinner has been a game changer for us, and like so much of what I'm grateful for in my life today, it started with a simple question right before I went to bed. I didn't know the answer, but I knew I wanted deeper friendships, and I knew this required a great question.

Lego Time is the metaphor I challenge you to consider as you approach your downtime. How will you play more with your family, spouse, and friends? How will you expand your network of friends and share your lives with others? People are designed for this, but our culture has shifted away from it. You must intentionally set out to create this connection with people, or your weekends will sink into the mundane and meaningless.

The Lego Time re-assessing question is all about how you can show up more fully in the lives of those you love and care for. But it also addresses your personal downtime. What are you doing for you so you can fully recharge and be present? You owe this to yourself, to your resucceed success, to God, and to those you love and care for.

QUESTIONS

Here are a few great Lego Time re-assessing questions to consider:

1. How can I improve my listening skills so that people I'm with know I'm present and attentive?

2. What mindset shift would it take for me to get down on the floor and actively play with my kids on Saturday morning? How would we all feel if I made this commitment?

3. What will it take for me to set aside personal time to recharge and reflect so I can be fully present with my family and friends for the rest of the weekend?

4. What areas of my life would benefit from personal coaching to clear the way to fully and authentically resucceed?

5. What are the two things I could do during our next vacation that would best set me up to return with passion, meaning, and fulfillment in my career and life?

In this section, I've shared more than 25 re-assess question examples. The questions focus on language, managing your energy, comfort zones, resistance, and Lego time, but I hope I've conveyed that the re-assess question helps you evaluate where you are now to determine your point A so that you can reach for point B: fulfillment and resucceeding.

You don't have to ask all these questions each week. This is a guide to help you get started. The goal is to ask a re-assess question right before you go to bed and await the answer. Experiment with the questions and craft your own so you can discern what you need to discover to live the life that is calling you. The questions just point you in the re-assess direction.

In the next section, I unpack the re-engage question. The re-engage questions are about instituting a new level of actionable results to your life by focusing on what's most important. I think you will enjoy the process of engaging in fresh ways with your life, the people in it, and yourself.

SPECIAL FREE BONUSES

5-MINUTE EPIC EVENING RITUAL

A Handy Reference for Those
Committed to Resucceeding

To download a comprehensive PDF of the entire 5-Minute Epic Evening Ritual, including sample questions, bedtime "ramp down" success routines, and tips and tricks, simply go to www.jamescolburn.net/resources.

FREE FAST LAUNCH PACKAGE

Give the Gift of Resucceeding

Many readers find the Resucceed system and the 5-Minute Epic Evening Ritual such a transformational process that they want to share it with those they love and care for. To help you help them, I have created what I call the "Free Fast Launch Package," which you can obtain by visiting www.jamescolburn.net/resources. By selecting the "Free Fast Launch Package," you can send your friends and loved ones the following for FREE:

- Three chapters of *Resucceed: Create an Extraordinary Future While You Sleep by Using the 5-Minute Epic Evening Ritual*

- FREE 5-Minute Epic Evening Ritual PDF Checklist

- FREE Training Videos and Audio on how to implement and immediately begin to Resucceed

I coach successful people to Resucceed. This is the answer to the call of my life. Each of us are called to fully "show up" in life with our unique brand and platform. My role in this is to help you bring forward hidden opportunities while exposing self-imposed limitations that hold you back. Seeing that light go on is my purpose. So much so, my logo is a light bulb.

All my coaching is done over the phone. This is by design to remove the typical obstacles to understanding. In most cases, you will never meet with me in person, which allows for a more meaningful, transparent coaching experience. Both coach and client find this helpful in the sharing and vulnerability that is necessary to resucceed.

I coach only highly successful, already-achieved individuals who seek to resucceed by adding fulfillment, meaning, passion, joy, and purpose to their lives.

Hire me when you seek one or more of the following:

- Emphatic desire to significantly increase your personal income

- Success that goes beyond what you have accepted and tolerated in your current brand of success

- Unquenchable interest in the 5-minute **Epic Evening Ritual** and how it can transform your life

- Profound new entrepreneurial startup that requires a new mindset and approach

- Energy management to get the most out of your work and play

- Clarification of purpose and strengths, and from this understanding, movement to the next level of success

My coaching clients have little to no patience for a long, drawn-out process, so my coaching agreements are never for longer than six months or more often than three times per month. My coaching clients come to me when they are absolutely ready to resucceed.

If you'd like to set up a personal 15 minute phone call with me, simply go to www.jamescolburn.net/coaching and follow the prompt to "Schedule a FREE 15-Minute Call." From there you will be directed to my scheduling application.

SECTION III

Re-Engage

Essentialism is not about how to get more things done; it's about how to get the right things done. It doesn't mean just doing less for the sake of less either. It is about making the wisest possible investment of your time and energy in order to operate at our highest point of contribution by doing only what is essential.

—GREG MCKEOWN

Next, I want to introduce you to the re-engage question of the 5-Minute Epic Evening Ritual. To engage is to bring into operation, enlist, or commission a great work. And this great work is *you*. Asking the re-engage question allows you to align with what is essential in your life, to open yourself to the great work that has yet to appear. You'll find different types of re-engaging questions that will help you do that: first things first, reflect, enoughness, echo, and digest. This is a critical part of resucceeding and provides the space for awareness in the present moment.

The re-engage question of your 5-Minute Epic Evening Ritual is an opportunity for deep personal reflection. The great part is that, like all the resucceed inquiries, you need only ask the question and let your creative mind, through the subconscious and the miraculous, do the work while you sleep. Approach these questions as special moments to engage with all areas of your life.

CHAPTER 13

FIRST THINGS FIRST

*What's the ONE thing you can do such that by doing it
everything else would be easier or unnecessary?*

—GARY KELLER AND JAY PAPASAN

The first-things-first inquiry is the practice of capturing your own attention and determining where you should focus. Reclaiming your attention isn't easy because, as life marches on, your roles and responsibilities intensify and your success and achievement take hold. The competition for your time and energy is fierce, and you dilute your ability to make an impact when you try to serve too many masters.

The first-things-first question is a great way to begin each week. I ask this question on Sunday evening. As I kneel by my nightstand, I consider the question that will help me focus on what's most important for the week ahead. I feel a wonderful peace come over me when I give myself permission to narrow my priorities to just one thing. It's freeing to realize that success in most areas of life boils down to a few defining, first-things-first activities and questions.

Once as a young father, I stood in line with my three-year-old son waiting for a cashier at Nordstrom. In front of us was an older man with a great smile, and he seemed to want to talk with me. You may have experienced this situation when you can tell someone wants to talk with you, but they don't know how to start. I wrestled with the equal but different challenge of deciding if I would help him or if I would watch him struggle. For some reason, I felt compelled to talk, and I'm so glad I did.

"Great day," I said to the man the next time he glanced at me.

"Sure is," he replied. "You've got a great boy there."

I thanked him as I patted my son Eliot on the shoulder. "He sure is."

"I remember having little kids like him," he said. "I remember feeling so responsible. Shoot, if I knew then what I know now. What I learned is that kids are like bank accounts, and the currency was how what I did made them feel. The most important gift I gave my children was how they felt when they were with me. Not what I bought or did with them, but how they felt."

This was a first-things-first moment for me. This man's approach to relating to his children was through an intangible feeling. Not something you could hold or point to, but rather a feeling that his children experienced. An honorable engagement. This moment also taught me to be willing to "engage" with someone I don't know. What he said forced me to look at relationships and connections through a different lens.

As you consider your first-things-first question, think of the areas of your life that seem cluttered and in need of simplicity or prioritization. For me back then, my new role as father felt cluttered, confusing, and overwhelming. I didn't know how I could use my time and energy to best care for my family. This man simplified the focus for me in a few short sentences. Sure, I could feel overwhelmed by the responsibility, but I could also remember that parenthood comes down to how my children feel when they are with me. This can happen for you too, but it begins with asking a great question about what's most important to you.

Consider the clutter and confusion in the most near and dear parts of your life. Then petition your creative mind and the miraculous for help to refine and distill your first-things-first focus so that you can simplify your approach to the essential one thing you can do ... now.

QUESTIONS

Here are a few re-engage first-things-first questions to get you started.

1. "What's the ONE thing *I* can do *tomorrow* such that by doing it everything else would be easier or unnecessary?" (Adapted from Gary Keller and Jay Papasan's *The One Thing*).

2. What is the first-things-first priority I can focus on around _____ to transform how my success would feel? For example, what if the first-things-first question related to your business explored your *why* instead of your next transaction, task, deadline, or to-do list?

3. What is the most powerful yet intangible way I can show my love to _____ so they will remember it for a lifetime?

4. How would it transform me to share my most important life lesson with a stranger tomorrow?

5. What is the most important thing I can do immediately upon waking tomorrow that will start the next week off right?

QUICK TAKEAWAY

Stop right now.

Sure, you can continue to read on, but draw a line in the sand in your mind and stop the chatter for a moment with me. Ask yourself, what is my first-things-first priority? Seek the defining focus that will lead you to be the inspiring person you were meant to be. In the quiet of your mind, explore whether you can influence the lives of others in certain areas by sharing your *one thing* or first-things-first focus. Perhaps the core value you hold dear is something someone else needs to hear. Be the "critical thing that's missing" for someone else today, just as the man in the store was for me, and you will watch your life transform. You will resucceed because you help others resucceed.

In the next chapter, I give you permission to daydream. In fact, I insist you schedule it. Sound good? You'll be amazed at what daydreaming can do to help you resucceed.

CHAPTER 14

REFLECTION

Without reflection, we go blindly on our way,
creating more unintended consequences,
and failing to achieve anything useful.

—MARGARET J. WHEATLEY

Reflection is a form of controlled daydreaming, and it may surprise you when I encourage you to not only allow this practice in your day, but to schedule it along with other mission-critical activities. I'll show you why this is so important, but first I want to identify what I mean by daydreaming.

In the book *Ungifted: Intelligence Redefined*, Scott Barry Kaufman describes three general types of daydreaming: (1) poor-attention control daydreaming, (2) guilty-dysphoric daydreaming, and (3) positive-constructive daydreaming. The reflective process of the resucceed system uses positive-constructive daydreaming, in which we "choose to disengage from external tasks" and allow our minds to make connections between the past, present, and future and explore meaning.

Reflection is rarely valued in the busyness of our culture, and the successful person spends far too little of life in this pursuit. Upon successful completion of a task, people say, "Next!" while skipping the cathartic time to reflect. People say with shallow breaths, "I'm only as good as my next sale," and that applies across the board to the next client, next book, next PTA meeting, and so on.

Reflection in the form of constructive daydreaming seems reserved for childhood, that time when people experience fewer hard limits. I remember fondly watching life happen outside the classroom windows for hours while in elementary school, only to be snapped back to the reality of a history lesson or math problem by the teacher calling on me: "Jimmy?"

But what if we need constructive daydreaming? What if reflection allowed you to see opportunities you hadn't yet considered? Would that be helpful?

I remember reading about a businessman's practice of spending one hour per day looking out his office window at the city below as a form of positive-constructive daydreaming. He intentionally scheduled time to explore ideas, celebrate wins, and feel the results of the positive decisions he had yet to make or engage with. His daydreaming was essential to his success because he tapped into an unconscious evaluation process that helped him filter, prioritize, and inspire the trajectory of his career and personal life. Because it was important, he scheduled this activity. How many of us schedule daydreaming? Is it true, as Plato is credited with saying, that "the unexamined life is not worth living"?

The re-engage reflection question is more of a precursor because you ask it to define the areas of your life and career that most deserve reflection and thoughtful consideration the next day. Before you ask the question, you must be willing to schedule time for constructive daydreaming. Perhaps an hour is a stretch for you, but how about five or ten minutes (while driving, shaving, or showering) to let your mind wander while considering a certain topic? Once you agree to do that, even if you don't know when you might find the time, you can seek the topic that deserves your reflection. I find that, even without reminding myself, I begin at the prescribed time if I set it in motion the night before with a great question.

I live in Seattle, and I spend a lot of time in traffic. This is the perfect time for reflection. Before bed, I challenge myself to reflect on what is most essential and necessary in my life right now. By asking a great re-engage reflection question, I seek guidance to learn which areas of my life—career, friendships, struggles—need reflection. I want to unlock the areas of my life that I have not yet considered important to reflect on. I wait to be amazed and surprised by the answer. It's exciting to go to sleep not knowing the answer but trusting that it is on its way to me.

In the morning, I take time to reflect when I warm up on the treadmill. I've learned over the years that I improve the quality of my reflection when I move. A rich topic for me is limiting beliefs. I play a game in which I try to uncover every limiting belief I can. It's a game, but it's also my reflection time. It starts with asking the re-engage reflection question the night before and setting up constructive daydreaming time in advance.

QUESTIONS

Here are five re-engage reflection questions to get you started. Approach these with curiosity. Be excited for the mystery to unfold while you sleep and the answer to arrive during your chosen period for reflection.

1. What area of my life or work deserves my thoughtful reflection tomorrow morning while I'm in the shower before I create an action plan?

2. While in traffic on the freeway tomorrow, what friendship or business relationship should I spend some time reflecting on?

3. Is there a certain way I interact with my family members that deserves reflection so I don't prevent closeness and connection?

4. Where do I miss opportunities to reflect on success in my business and with the people I work with that would allow for further growth and development?

5. What is one time during my work days that I could use consistently to reflect on something I have never considered?

> **QUICK TAKEAWAY**
>
> Tonight, craft a re-engage reflection question that challenges you to uncover an area you should consider for further reflection. Decide when and where you will do this reflection the next day. Write it down. Go to sleep. Tomorrow, during your chosen time, remind yourself of the reflection question. When the answer arrives, and it will, reflect on it.

Constructive daydreaming is a key aspect of resucceeding, and the topic of the next chapter amplifies this. Overcoming the false belief that I wasn't enough has changed every area of my life. The sweetest part is that you have very little to do with your enoughness.

CHAPTER 15

ENOUGHNESS

An inevitable though often ignored dimension of the quest
for "wholeness" is that we must embrace what we dislike
or find shameful about ourselves as well as what
we are confident and proud of.

—PARKER J. PALMER

Many people I know struggle with the debilitating effects of feeling as if they are not enough. And what's interesting is that if someone acts as though they are enough, most likely, deep down inside, they don't believe it. This deep sense of inadequacy causes many people to chase approval in all forms from others. Perhaps they hope to earn their way into a "club of enoughness," as if success and achievement are the dues to obtain a membership card. It makes sense then that investigating your sense of enoughness is a critical component of resucceeding.

In chapter 4, I mentioned how you need to get disgusted with the lie that you are not enough if you want to resucceed. In this chapter, I want to further unpack this lack of enoughness. To move beyond survival success, you must understand the power this belief has over you and learn to use it for your transformation and growth.

You might remember the story of me in the duck yard and how I promised to protect my mother from any hurt or pain, especially hurts that came from my brother's and father's addictions. In recent years, I realized that by making the offer, I had signed up for too much because I couldn't fully protect my mom from this and many other hurts that would come along. My brother's addiction continued until he took his own life, and my dad's alcoholism contributed to the decline of my parents' 55-year marriage. I had no control over how my dad and brother behaved, nor could I change how my mother responded to their actions or any other future hurts.

It's no surprise that I spent so much of my life trying to protect my mother. This is what it looks like to chase the need to feel and be enough. And there was no way for me to win that game.

Enoughness comes from what we believe or what we have accepted as true in our life. At some point, someone told us (or we told ourselves) and we accepted as true the story that we aren't enough in some or all areas of our life. The first step in unraveling this false belief is to go back to the day when things changed and rewrite the story. When I work with people on enoughness, it is amazing how quickly they remember when they heard or decided that they were not enough. It's waiting for you if you'll stay curious and open.

Here's the truth: we are all are enough. Better put, you are absolutely, 100 percent, irrefutably enough. And yet most of us at one point accepted that we aren't enough and acted upon it.

It's time to take back the truth, not by willpower, but because we are enough despite ourselves. Despite our humanness, despite any bad decisions we've made, despite our physical, emotional, and mental limitations. No work is required here. You are enough, period! You were enough the moment you made your first noise in the hospital room after your birth. Ultimately, you are enough because God wonderfully created you.

The great part is that the state of being enough has nothing to do with you. It's independent of you or anything you can do. If it feels as if I'm repeating this, you're right, and here's why: Believing you are enough is critical to resucceeding. And it's such a simple concept we can skip over it. You've repeated the negative story ad nauseam; it has traction. I want to help you get positive momentum to embrace the truth.

I discovered a clue that pointed to this truth when my dad had a heart attack while I was in college almost 600 miles from home. I jumped on the first plane out of town. Before the end of the day, I was at my dad's bedside in the intensive care unit in Medford, Oregon. It seemed that everything would be okay if my dad changed his eating and exercise habits, which we told him was nonnegotiable.

The next morning, my mom and I attended a local country church called Applegate Christian Fellowship. I remember one key part of the pastor's sermon that changed my views on life (and death) and whether I was enough.

The pastor said that life and our desire to be adequate (or enough) is a lot like being in the Olympics. The difference, he said, is in how we win the gold medal. "Imagine you've won the semifinals and you're warming up on the sidelines for the competition of your life. Your coach runs up to you and says, 'I've got something I need to tell you. You've done such an amazing job in the semifinals that you have already won the finals. No matter what happens or what you do next, you've already won the gold.'" The pastor was speaking to the unmerited grace that God gives everyone. As Ephesians 2:8 reminds us "it is by grace you have been saved, through faith—and this is not from yourselves, it is the gift of God."

Friends, whatever your faith, whatever your beliefs, the fact is you cannot and will not *earn* your way into a place of fully justified existence, prominence, purpose, and meaning. It does not happen that way. There are parts of your life and even your success that you didn't make happen. You were simply enough.

This is the enoughness I'm talking about. Through practice, you will grow in your ability to examine your life's pursuit, the success you chase and enjoy, and why you do what you do. You also will come to know that much of your fervor for success comes from your desire to be enough. Examine what you seek and ask yourself if what you truly want is to earn your way to being enough. In case you're worried, believing you are enough won't rob you of your drive to be successful. You will add meaning and purpose as fuel for your pursuit, instead of pursuing success to make up a deficit. This is the art of resucceeding.

When I hired the coach who taught me about playing Legos with my kids, I told her how I needed to keep my feet to the fire so I wouldn't lose the edge that kept me successful. One way I kept my edge was by investing or spending my money. The last thing I wanted was a bunch of money in my checking account. Sound familiar? You'd think it would make me comfortable or reduce my stress, but it did quite the opposite.

As a highly successful individual, you understand the tension that comes from *having enough*. Maybe you think it dulls your edge, your ability to be successful, because you *need enough* pressure. The thinking is that if you don't live in a state of lack, you won't have reason to pursue achievement.

My coach explained that she thought the edge I spoke of was *fear*. I had created a fear-based purpose to keep my hands to the plow of my success. She said, "Fear becomes a negative fuel. The fear helped you focus in the beginning, but over time, it tears you down, freezes you out, and capsizes your success."

In which part of your life don't you feel enough? You'll find it in those things you recklessly chase for legitimacy and acknowledgement. Those things you think would be lost if you let go of fear and accept that you are enough.

I can't say this often enough because the mistaken belief has such power over us. The enoughness question helps you break through your resistance and old patterns of thought to make what is invisible in your life visible, not for others, but for you. You can take the daily-grind blinders off and see the miraculous that has been in front of you the whole time. Your enoughness is not about you or what you do. You are complete and enough in spite of yourself.

You can recognize the miraculous in the job interview that didn't land you the job, but that opened your mind to self-reflection, better clarity, direction, and a sincere understanding of what you want versus what you think you must do.

You'll see the beauty of connecting with others. Not only your family, but in allowing others to share in your life. To be known. Not putting that off for another decade when you're less busy, but doing it now because the next decade may never arrive.

Learn to recognize enoughness while sitting and watching the trees sway in the breeze and the sky moving past. The melody of it all. Falling in love with the something that is found in the not doing, but being and noticing. Not chasing it, but simply allowing.

Observe your enoughness in the tough questions about why you do what you do: the "what for" questions surrounding our motivations for the things we do and assign our identity to. What *is* the truth behind our endless need for busyness—that's the invisible made visible. Like discovering why we check email and social media before our feet hit the ground in the morning and last thing at night. Why do we schedule coffee with a good friend and then distance ourselves with a laptop lid or some other device?

We become complete by no longer accepting busyness at the expense of true connection. Not only connection to others, but with ourselves, and, better yet, our Creator.

It would be easy to discount the art of becoming complete as emotional nonsense compared to the larger concerns at hand, like making and retaining money. But I'm here to remind you that your *enoughness* is not related to the money you make or the success you chase. I argue that falling for the lie that your fear of loss or inadequacy will drive your success is unfounded. Fear truly is a negative fuel. The more fear you pack on, the less you will achieve, and surely the less money you will retain.

Ever had someone challenge you to become complete? Well, now you have! But I won't stop there because helping others resucceed is part of my calling. The freedom to pursue purpose and success is high octane fuel that burns clean.

Tony Robbins once said, "If I follow the trail of your stress, it will take me to your deepest fears. And I always believe that life is the dance between what you desire most and what you fear most."

For some, the desire to be enough is found in the ability to show people they can be successful even when no one else thinks so. For others, the desire to be enough is an ill-formed response to the words said and told years before: "You won't amount to anything" or "You can't do that! You're too short" or "You're not smart enough."

Even if you disagree with me, you are enough. Regardless of what you tell yourself or me, you are enough. It is something you haven't earned but has been freely given. In the moment you were born, you were enough. You are enough because God is enough. If you contend that you are not enough, then you are saying that God is not enough.

Some might say, "I don't believe in God," to which I respond, "Okay, do you believe in the universe? If you say you are not enough, then the universe from which you came is not enough." God is how I explain how I came to be here, but you can call it what you like. Your *enoughness* doesn't come from you. It is given freely by your existence. Like it or not, that's the secret.

As I sat in Applegate Christian Fellowship with my mom while my dad recovered in the hospital, I realized just how much I had been trying to earn my way into being enough. Of course, our culture and the people who inhabit our world don't help much with that. Bosses, parents, spouses, and children say and do things that evoke the feeling that we are not enough. We're not the only ones caught in this fearsome cycle. Worse is what we say to ourselves as we internalize and perpetuate the belief. But it's a lie, and that's what we must overcome if we are going to resucceed.

That is not all there is to resucceeding in this area. Just as I am showing you that you are enough, I challenge you to do the same for others. Although I've explained that external validation has little to do with our enoughness, there is a tremendous value in reminding those you care about that they are enough. You can observe them change in obvious and subtle ways as they take the message onboard. By telling others that they too are enough, you remind yourself. We all need this in a world that repeatedly tells us we are not.

QUESTIONS

Here are several questions you can ask to investigate your enoughness. My goal for you is to uncover all the reasons you already are enough. Once you realize that you are truly enough, you will become unstoppable because you won't be at the mercy of the voice in your head that uses fear as fuel.

1. Where in my life do I fail to show up fully and believe I don't have what it takes because I think I must earn my right to be enough?

2. Who in my life deserves for me to tell them they are enough, not because of what they do for me or others, but because they are simply enough?

3. In what area of my life do I need to let go of the not-enough persona I have accepted or adopted for myself?

4. If I believed I was enough in the area of _____, how would I show up differently?

5. How do I fail to show up in social situations because I don't feel I am enough when I would be more attractive and engaging if I changed my thinking?

The fifth question is special for me because I realized through the 5-Minute Epic Evening Ritual and my great questions that I was walking around with a straight face, not because I was serious, but because I didn't feel I was enough to smile. Somehow I felt that others were happier than I was. I would walk around with my shoulders hunched and a frown on my face.

One morning, after asking the question about failing to show up, the answer arrived that I was enough to smile and hold my shoulders back and my head up. This wasn't arrogance, but a response to recognizing that I am more than enough, that I'm enough because God is enough, and that it is my responsibility to show it to others.

QUICK TAKEAWAY

Take a moment to go back in time to that moment when you either heard that you weren't enough or told yourself you weren't enough. If it doesn't come to you right away, open yourself up to remembering it. To help jog your memory, when was it that you no longer believed you could do anything if you put your mind to it? When was the moment someone lectured you, made you sit on the sidelines, gave you a bad grade, or told you that achievement in a certain area couldn't or wouldn't be yours?

In what area of your life do you try to control things to prove your enoughness? What happened when you were younger that made you want to prove this to others?

Now that you have worked through your enoughness, it's time to let others know. In the next chapter, I teach you what it means to echo your life to others.

CHAPTER 16

ECHO

You are a child of God. Your playing small does not serve the world. There is nothing enlightened about shrinking so that other people will not feel insecure around you. We are all meant to shine, as children do. We were born to make manifest the glory of God that is within us. It is not just in some of us; it is in everyone and as we let our own light shine, we unconsciously give others permission to do the same. As we are liberated from our own fear, our presence automatically liberates others.

—MARIANNE WILLIAMSON

I use the word echo as a metaphor for letting others in the world—your family, your friends, those you have influence over—hear what you are up to, what you believe in, and the things that you are passionate about. To echo is to let your life speak to others and let it be known. For me, writing this book is to echo my life. It is the expression of my calling.

When we make an echo, we emit a noise that reverberates off something and returns to us. The process of echoing our life requires that we let our life speak loud enough for others to hear, allowing ourselves to be known, and staying open to hear the echo's return, a confirmation of how it was received and how it contributed to the lives of others.

I could close this chapter by telling you to take Marianne Williamson's quote to heart. It is a powerful statement: As we shine our light, we give others permission to do the same.

But my history with this quote goes deeper.

A few years ago, I included the above quote in my email signature. Each time I drafted a new message, I would ask myself, should I leave the quote at the bottom for this recipient? I decided on a case-by-case basis whether the recipient deserved or could handle the quote, or more to the point, if my affiliation with the quote might be misconstrued or show weakness.

After my inner dialogue about one such email to a new client, I left the quote in my signature and then hit send.

My client responded right away: "Anyone who would risk placing that quote in their email signature is someone I could only hope to work with."

My heart warmed at her response, but I immediately reread the quote and realized that, by deleting it depending on the recipient, I had been "playing small." I was choosing not to echo. My new client had taught me a valuable lesson. Don't play small to make others feel comfortable. We aren't called to do this. We are called to be bold! We are called to echo our truth, our life.

The longer I'm on this earth interacting with humans, the more I realize that what we want from each other is authenticity. Our strength is found not in making others feel comfortable, but instead through our clarity and ability to shine our light in the world. This is our echo.

Don't shrink! Be vulnerable!

Are you willing to echo? Are you willing to tell the world in your own unique, authentic way that you are enough?

QUESTIONS

The following are a few great echo questions for you to consider. The goal is to uncover the ways you can echo your life and share your light with friends, colleagues, your community, and the world. Once we realize that we are enough despite ourselves, it's time to echo our truth.

1. What is something I believe I must share with the world that I have avoided doing to make others feel comfortable?

2. What are some unique ways I can echo my life's calling to others tomorrow that will help me further accept my enoughness?

3. How can I encourage the people I encounter tomorrow to echo their lives in ways that contribute to others?

4. What is something I have always wanted to do, and that would allow me to share my essence, that I avoid out of fear that others won't accept it or me?

5. Are there areas of my life in which I already echo that
   I should expand now that I know that I am absolutely,
   100 percent enough?

Your echo is your platform. You were designed to show up,
contribute, and let your life speak to others.

QUICK TAKEAWAY

I urge you to explore the areas of your life where you shrink
to make others feel more comfortable. The things you
consider doing but then don't. I often think of ways I could
be more generous, but I fail to follow through because I
fear how it will be perceived or if I will be accepted. As I
examine echoing in my life, I realize there is no room for
shrinking. We arrive here on earth with divine gifts, found
within our purpose, that no one else possesses. The gift
comes with the responsibility to echo and share with the
world. It is not only for you that the gift exists, but for your
fellow humans. Resucceeding helps you identify the areas
in your life that you are responsible to echo.

Now that you know how to echo and send your light into
the world, I show you one more re-engage question, the art
and process of digesting, and the simple system I created to
assimilate and engage with what you take in.

CHAPTER 17

DIGEST

*What if we stopped celebrating being busy as a measurement
of importance? What if instead we celebrated how much
time we had spent listening, pondering, meditating,
and enjoying time with the most important
people in our lives?*

—GARY MCKEOWN

In a world where the pursuit of knowledge is a given (whether
we need or want it), we desperately need to learn to digest
and assimilate the content we take in. To be fully alive and
resucceed requires that we become skilled at integrating what
we learn.

In the last year, I listened to 40 books. With my travel schedule, I've learned to love audiobooks. One day, I failed to engage with and assimilate what I had been learning. This process is what I call digesting. With information coming at us from all directions, it's easy to get lost in the consumption of material and forget to do something with it. Information gathering for its own sake does not serve us or help us resucceed.

Success literature often tells us that the people we keep company with and the books we read define us. But the question remains, what are we doing to deepen our connections and engage with what we learn?

With the re-engage digest question, I urge you to explore what happens after you connect with others or pursue knowledge. Are you exploring or even questioning the validity of what you learn? Are you putting it to work in your life? Do you take action?

"Shelf esteem" is a term in the urban dictionary that describes "when someone builds their self-esteem from self-help books." It's great to read and open ourselves up to new ideas, but it does no good to read self-help books and never assimilate or integrate what you've learned.

In my quest for learning through reading, I found myself looking for the next book before I had finished the current one. Instead of taking time to digest what I'd read, I was on to the next one.

In response to this, I implemented a rule that, for the first 10 days of the month, I can read or listen to books, podcasts, TED Talks, YouTube videos, etc. The remaining days of the month, I engage with the material, try it on for size, and discuss it with others in my community. This allows me to take in new ideas, discuss them with others, and test and integrate the best of what I've learned. I believe deeply in the value of learning and connecting, and my system supports me in doing both in a disciplined manner. It might not work for you, but I had to put some limits on my pursuit of more to find the kernel of truth and the beauty of relationships with others around knowledge.

The re-engage digest question challenges you to take time to incorporate and process what you have learned before moving on to something new.

In what areas of your life do you need to digest more of what you've learned? Perhaps it's a great conversation with a friend, a book that moved you, a movie that spoke to you, or a thought-provoking sermon at church. If all we do is accumulate and never grow, what good is it?

Now consider what you allow to accumulate. Is it the friends you keep, the books you read, the knowledge you harbor? Do you leave space between moments of accumulation for growth and evolution? The practice of digesting what you've learned is critical to resucceeding.

QUESTIONS

The following are a few great questions you might ask to better digest what you learn. The goal is to discover where you have skipped applying the lesson in pursuit of more knowledge.

1. Have I pondered the books I've read and loved? How can I carry what is meaningful with me?

2. Are there people who have showed up in my life that I can learn from that I have avoided?

3. What is something I have learned that I can put into practice to improve my life starting tomorrow?

4. In what area of my life do I consume knowledge without giving myself time to integrate what I have learned?

5. What is a constructive way I can build time in my schedule to assimilate and engage with what I have learned?

For the successful individual, more information, new information, and better information is power. But even more powerful is the ability to digest what we've learned and connect with those we know.

QUICK TAKEAWAY

Tonight, craft your re-engage digest question to receive creative ways to better digest what you learn and connect with those you know. Consider scheduling a regular time and place to do this. This simple technique will deepen and broaden your ability to act and authentically resucceed.

Now you have five different types of re-engage questions to help you focus on what's important in life: your great work in the world. Each night, before you go to bed, ask the re-engage question of your choice—one I've shared or one you've written. Remember that it is in asking and waiting for the answer that you will find yourself more fully engaging in your own life, with those you know, what you learn, and how you share it with the world.

It's time to reveal the third and final question of the 5-Minute Epic Evening Ritual: Re-affirm. This question has a twist: It's about what you already know about yourself but rarely explore. I love this question because it feels like a soft blanket to me. And it should because you ask it right before you pull the soft blanket up to your shoulders and go to sleep. Get ready to re-affirm.

SECTION IV

Re-Affirm

To create is to defy emptiness. It is generous, it affirms. To make is to add to the world, not subtract from it.

—CHARLOTTE WOOD

You can't go far as a successful individual without understanding the value of affirmations. In fact, affirmations are a buzzword in the self-help community, and people incorporate them in success rituals. In the resucceed context, to affirm is to believe, state your dedication, and enunciate your cause.

The re-affirm question is the third and final one you will craft during your 5-Minute Epic Evening Ritual each evening right before you go to sleep. Although it is the final question, it is not the least important. In fact, all three questions—re-assess, re-engage, and re-affirm—hold equal weight in the resucceed system.

I place this question last because re-affirming deals with noticing and acknowledging what we already have, instead of what we hope to gain. So much of the time, and especially as a successful person, acknowledging what we have falls by the wayside as we push for more and forget what we already enjoy.

When we affirm, we seek and discover our core values—what we already possess. Whatever they may be, these values direct our steps, even when we don't realize what they are. We can further their impact and allow them to guide our steps and decisions when we stay conscious of them. Then we open ourselves to making our core values evident to our family, friends, community, and perhaps also the world. Re-affirming our core values is a process of discovering and revealing.

Every evening, I'm excited to get to the third question because I look forward to deepening my understanding of my core values. I can better understand who I am, what is most important to me, how I view the world, how I define success, and who I hope to become. As I grow in understanding, I learn what drives me to take the actions I take. Not every event will communicate as clearly as my Costco incident did in what motivated me in the moment, but when I ask re-affirm questions, I gain clarity.

Even highly successful people don't always understand why they do what they do. For many, the trap of success forces them into autopilot where they forget to clarify their core values. They become so busy and lost in the highly visible aspects of their success—the accolades, the trappings, the title, the income—they forget to clarify how their success ties in with their core values. It's a bigger challenge than it seems. The pursuit of success without values deprives people of their steady North Star to navigate difficult waters and make tough decisions. Never mind enjoying the journey. Success and achievement, without a clear understanding of our core values, leaves us wanting more even at the pinnacle of our success.

I once asked a well-known author and past president of a successful Fortune 500 company about how he'd come to a decision that others within the business community openly questioned. His answer was simple: "I live by a certain set of core values. The decision was easy because it fell in line with these core values. That's the best way I have to explain it." Despite the criticism of others, he was at peace with himself and his decision because he understood how it related to his North Star.

In this section, I'll unpack what it means to re-affirm. The re-affirm question focuses on the following five areas: becoming, moments of brilliance, the miraculous, granular gratitude, and celebration.

This process is powerful. The inquiry goes to the very heart of our purpose, core values, and North Star.

If you are ready to learn about the third and final great question of the resucceed system, first, you must realize that you have a strategic purpose. Figuring out what this is becomes the starting point for all you do, seek, and contribute. Do you believe you have a strategic purpose here on earth? I'm here to tell you that you do.

CHAPTER 18

BECOMING

Learn to get in touch with the silence within yourself, and know that everything in life has purpose. There are no mistakes, no coincidences, all events are blessings given to us to learn from.

—ELISABETH KUBLER-ROSS

Most people seek to arrive somewhere. Life for them is like a long airplane trip, but this journey moves them toward an obscure destination in the future where they think they will feel complete, content, and whole. The re-affirm question helps you shift your mindset to view your life as a process of becoming more *You.*

I remember when a friend and past employer told me, "Jimmy, it seems you are in a race to somewhere, but what happens when you get there?" He might not have realized the power of his question or the impact it had on me. I don't think I did either at the time, but today the question resonates with me through re-affirming.

Becoming presents a different focus: we no longer aim for an elusive finish line, but instead work toward becoming a clearer version of ourselves. It takes special care to remove the disguises we wear in public. First, we must recognize the public persona, our "game face," or our "business side." We don't have to wear different hats depending on the stage we stand on in the moment. We put energy into figuring out who we are, what truly moves us, why we take action, and which areas in our lives take from us instead of support our mission.

The re-affirm question that you ask right before you go to sleep is your chance to explore areas of your life where you still are not clear, but want to know more.

The other day I listened to an online coach who spoke about what he was working on in his own life: how he showed up in his family. He questioned the way he listened to his wife and children, how he engaged in the conversation and contributed to the family, even when he was exhausted from work or pre-occupied with stress. He was curious and open to becoming a better version of himself at home with his family.

Becoming is the process of self-evolution from who you are today to who you could be, a better, more accurate version of yourself. The re-affirm becoming question is like a timeout you give yourself to reveal areas where you need to become that better and more accurate version of yourself.

QUESTIONS

1. If I had to know what my strategic purpose is tomorrow, what would I need to see or know better?

2. How can I move toward my true self and become more of who I already am, starting tomorrow?

3. In what area of my life am I focused on arriving at a destination instead of becoming a better version of myself?

4. Is there an area of my life that I resist sharing with others (what I think, who I am deep inside) for fear of how I will be received?

5. When I imagine becoming a better and more accurate version of myself, what area of my life is ready for the upgrade?

We all are in the process of becoming. Even in our final hours on earth, a great work is in progress. The re-affirm becoming question points you to who you are and how that contributes to why you are here.

QUICK TAKEAWAY

Have you ever traveled to a new city where you knew no one? For me, there's something magical about being anonymous in a new place. No one knows your personal baggage, your bad decisions, what you do for a living, or who you are. When I travel, I use this anonymous time to wonder what I would become if the slate were clean and I had nothing from the past to lean on or allow to hold me back. What jumps out at me is how others perceive me or the labels that others have assigned to me is what holds me back the most from becoming a more accurate version of myself.

Take a moment and ask yourself who you would become if you landed in a new city with a clean slate. Your answer to this question will give you a glimpse of the person you want to become, who you are that is trying to come through. The trick, however, is to respond and let go of the mental constraints to push forward on your process of becoming. The re-affirming becoming question begins your moment of discovery in the areas of your life where you have yet to become.

You don't have to be anonymous or wait for a trip to a new city. You can become the best version of you *now*. Just as George Eliot said, "It is never too late to be what you might have been." What's interesting is that George Eliot was really Mary Ann Evans. She adopted a male pen name because she wanted her words and not her gender to matter to the reader. She embodied the concept that it is never too late to be what you might have been—a serious author who questioned the traditional roles of the Victorian era—but also the tension that arises when you want to show the world who you are.

What is your pen name?

As you become a more accurate version of yourself, you'll want to become aware of your moments of brilliance. I write about this in the next chapter, along with the single biggest reason they are hard to recognize. Big or small, our moments of brilliance are building upon themselves, and it is our job to recognize them.

CHAPTER 19

MOMENTS OF BRILLIANCE

To live content with small means; to see elegance rather than luxury, and refinement rather than fashion; to be worthy, not respectable; and wealthy, not rich; to study hard, think quietly, talk gently, act frankly ... to listen to stars and buds, to babes and sages, with open heart; await occasions, hurry never ... this is my symphony.

—WILLIAM HENRY CHANNING

Integral to re-affirmation is the concept that each person here on earth is uniquely designed to have plentiful moments of brilliance. They aren't all earth-shattering, Wikipedia-worthy moments, but we experience moments of brilliance that shape who we are and that matter and contribute to others.

Consider the brilliant moment of Captain Chesley "Sully" Sullenberger III on January 15, 2009, when he conducted an emergency water landing of US Airways Flight 1549 on the Hudson River off Manhattan. You can be sure Captain Sullenberger had thought through the *what ifs* of emergency situations during flight, but outside of simulation training, he hadn't practiced a water landing.

When asked about this moment of brilliance, the pilot responded, "One way of looking at this might be that, for 42 years, I've been making small, regular deposits in this bank of experience: education and training. And on January 15, the balance was sufficient so that I could make a very large withdrawal."

This was brilliance. It happened not because Captain Sullenberger *made it happen*, but because he was *ready for it to happen*. One hundred fifty passengers and five crew members made it out alive and were deeply grateful for those regular deposits.

My question here is, what was more brilliant, the small incremental deposits of experience, education, and practice over a lifetime or the water landing on January 15? The answer that arose is that the brilliance was found in both in equal measure.

Captain Sullenberger's moment was spectacular and hard to miss. In our lives, it is far too easy to discount brilliant moments or not even notice them. The re-affirming question related to brilliance serves as a call to our subconscious and the miraculous to make our moments of brilliance noticeable, not so much to others, as to ourselves.

Airline pilots face life and death stakes to encourage their regular deposits, which is not to take anything away from

Captain Sullenberger's heroic actions. But not all of us manage the safety of hundreds of people when we go to work each day. Just the same, the re-affirm brilliance question highlights our daily deposits so that we acknowledge them for what they are. As we become aware of them, we also may notice how each one builds upon the prior deposit and leads, directs, and moves us in preparing our own version of brilliance.

The Hudson River landing is an example of ultimate brilliance. Moments of that magnitude are rare, and we might encounter only a few like this in our lives. It's unlikely that you'll land a commercial airplane on the Hudson River, but you make small, daily deposits to use someday for your ultimate moments of brilliance.

QUESTIONS

To re-affirm your deposits and moments of brilliance, you need only prompt yourself with a great question.

1. What are ways I make small deposits each day toward a future withdrawal?

2. How can I make more deposits in my daily life by letting go of the mental constraints I have set up for myself?

3. What are three brilliant deposits I have already contributed?

4. What is my own version of a "life and death" need for making small incremental deposits in my moments of brilliance account?

5. What would I love for my ultimate brilliant moment to be someday?

Remember, you are asking these questions before you go to bed. You aren't trying to answer them. Instead, you remain open to hearing the answer over time.

QUICK TAKEAWAY

One way to boost your ability to notice brilliant moments in your life is to look for them in someone else's life. Think for a moment about someone you love, your significant other or another special person in your life, and record the moments of brilliance you know they have accomplished already. If you are driving, just think of one and remember it.

Then think of a moment of brilliance in this person's life that you are fairly certain they aren't aware of, something they have discounted or might not see as brilliant the way everyone else does.

Once you answer these questions, go to that person and share what you have recalled about their moments of brilliance. Teach this special person what you have learned. Teach them the art of asking the re-affirm moment of brilliance question.

I'm excited to share what I call the miraculous, which shows up while you sleep and helps you answer your great questions. This is huge and your ability to stay open to this power in your sleep will be a game changer.

CHAPTER 20

THE MIRACULOUS

Ask and it will be given to you; seek and you will find;
knock and the door will be opened to you.

—MATTHEW 7:7

Men are never duly touched and impressed with a
conviction of their insignificance, until they have
contrasted themselves with the majesty of God.

—R.C. SPROUL

One morning I received a text from a previous coaching client and friend asking if I was in town. I told him that I would return the next day. A few minutes passed, and he didn't respond. It occurred to me that I rarely hear from this friend by text, and when I do, it is usually because there's something going on in his life that he really needs to talk to me about. To test my hunch, I asked him if he would like to meet. He replied quickly, "Yes!"

The next day we met for coffee, and only a couple minutes had passed when my friend explained that he'd received a job offer with great benefits and salary. But he would have to move his family. He felt lucky that this move would bring them closer to where he and his wife had met and gone to college together, a place with great memories for them.

My friend further explained that, although the job offer was great, he and his wife were struggling with the decision because he didn't feel ready to leave his current job. "This is a great opportunity," he said, "but my gut tells me it might've arrived a little too early for us." Aside from his loyalty to his current job, he explained that his kids and wife loved their neighborhood and hadn't expected to move away from it anytime soon.

As he explained his predicament, I realized that what he was really saying was that he didn't feel pulled to this new job, he felt pushed. There's a real difference between push and pull.

Being pushed into anything doesn't feel good, even if it's something we might appreciate at another time or something that "should" make us grateful. It's more akin to being manipulated. Survival success can mimic this sensation if we're tempted by a great opportunity or more money. As a kid, I remember being encouraged to jump off the high dive for the first time. I stood at the end of the board and sensed the impatience of the kids at the bottom of the ladder who were waiting for their turn. It was scary, disempowering, and I felt out of control.

When we feel pulled by a situation? That's different. It feels empowering, a strength beyond us, an unexplainable power moves us to another chapter, job, venture, or evolution of self. One of my coaches once described this pull as something you feel in your gut instead of your head. (The term no-brainer comes to mind.) Far from an intellectual decision or process, it moves you emotionally and physically to a new spot in your life.

As I sat with my friend, I decided that instead of telling him what I thought he should do, which he would experience as more pushing, I would challenge him to have an 5-Minute Epic Evening Ritual. I encouraged him to ask a great question right before bed and record it on a 3x5 card: What would it look like to feel a miraculous pull to a new job opportunity so much that I could do nothing but accept the position and move my family immediately? I suggested that he let his creative mind and the miraculous go to work while he slept on this big decision.

For most of this book, I've hinted at the power of the miraculous in our lives to help us during sleep and uncover answers to our great questions. In this chapter, I share exactly what the miraculous means to me and invite you to decide what it means for you. If it feels as if we're taking a turn toward the spiritual, you're right. I hope that wherever you are with your own personal faith beliefs, this explanation will help you understand how the miraculous shows up in your business and personal decisions.

Before I dive in, I want you to understand that my faith is my own, and I know that. Your spiritual beliefs and faith are yours. We do not have to agree on matters of faith for you to apply the resucceed system. That said, if I didn't share my position on this point, I would be leaving out a critical piece of the 5-Minute Epic Evening Ritual and what it means to resucceed. I can't hold this back and be authentic.

When I ask a great question before I go to sleep and remain open, I receive answers from the miraculous, as well as the creative mind. This is a real thing. The miraculous plays a huge role in the answers I receive, and others who have engaged with the resucceed system tell me they've had the same experience: The answers that arrive are from something outside of them and beyond their comprehension.

I believe that such answers arrive because we remain open to them, not because of a credo we have memorized, a prayer we have uttered, or whether we attended Sunday school as a child. If it seems as if help from the miraculous has disappeared from your life or become distant, it is my belief that God (the miraculous) has never shifted. Instead, we have moved or altered the connection, our proximity, or our belief. The resucceed system simply points us back to the miraculous accessed through our subconscious mind with answers to the great questions of our life that we ask. This is a critical component of the 5-Minute Epic Evening Ritual.

Although this is a book for those who are already successful, our success comes in many shapes and sizes. Success depends on how we define it, or what we believe success means to us. Because this belief plays such a pivotal role in our success, it isn't a far stretch to consider that our belief system reveals or conceals the answers to our great questions.

Today, my business success comes from the trust mentioned in 2 Corinthians 5:7: "For we live by faith, not by sight." It hasn't always been that way, let me tell you. I know now that my success has more to do with what I believe, and what's behind my eyes, than what I see or what I can intellectually construct for myself with my conscious mind. As hard as it might seem to trust something other than what's in front of your eyes, the resucceed system has proven time and time again that it's possible.

When you believe that the miraculous will show up and answer your great questions, the answers arrive. That might sound super simplistic, maybe even a bit woo-woo, but the great part is that it's a lot less about the questions you ask and a lot more about the fact that you believe that a power beyond you, a supernatural power, brings you answers to questions you can't yet answer.

The word miraculous refers to a supernatural power or agency: a power beyond our control. And yet it is our decision to open ourselves to it. Just as the epigraph at the beginning of this chapter, Matthew 7:7, mentions the supernatural power of our direct requests for the miraculous to show up in our lives: When we ask, seek, and knock, we're given knowledge, we find what we are looking for, and closed doors opened. In this way, we receive answers to our great questions.

The miraculous I mention in the 5-Minute Epic Evening Ritual and the answers to your great questions come from the same supernatural response to your willingness to listen. This ritual provides access to answers from your creative mind through the subconscious, answers you don't know you know, but also from a supernatural power, something beyond us, unseen and powerful in each of our lives.

My context of the supernatural is the Christian faith. You might have a different context. I believe that the answers I receive from the miraculous come directly from the Creator of the Universe. For me, all of life is miraculous. What you believe is your call. You can doubt that the miraculous plays a role in your life and the 5-Minute Epic Evening Ritual, but how does that benefit you?

Daniel G. Groody, the author of *Globalization, Spirituality and Justice*, writes of a life that honors the miraculous: "[Life is] more on being than having, on the quality of one's heart rather than the quantity of one's possessions, and on the value of inner beauty rather than outer appearance, those committed to a Gospel-motivated simplicity seek to look beyond the consumer creeds of contemporary culture in order [to] find what truly liberates."

Although I wasn't born to wealth, I have found financial success as an adult, and from this I've noticed a few things. What I've observed more than anything else is that wealth hasn't been the answer to the disorders of my heart. As much as I wanted money to solve my internal struggles, it did quite the opposite. If anything, my wealth masked my discontent, and the more wealth I enjoyed, the more I noticed the lies about money: that it could solve my problems, that it would fix me, that money is the magic bullet. I knew that the disorders inside me remained after trying to placate my struggle with the symbols of success that our society honors and respects.

The re-affirm miraculous question is based on our willingness to release the need to have all the answers. It's a surrender of control. By opening up to a miraculous intervention in your life, an intervention over your money, success and achievements, you will immediately experience answers to the deep and unanswered questions that you dare ask. Such an intervention will instruct you that what makes you great often is not you, but the overarching power of the supernatural in your life. What makes us great is that we aren't God.

In the quiet of the evening just before you go to sleep, the 5-minute Epic Evening Ritual challenges you to open to the miraculous in question form: posing great questions, for which you have no answers, to none other than the miraculous. The result of this discipline, this surrender, is that you will hear from the supernatural. Regardless of your religious background or lack thereof, or whether you believe God exists at all, the miraculous will show up while you sleep to deliver answers to your great questions if you let it.

Questions to the miraculous are personal, but it is important to know that they don't require careful phrasing or well-thought-out sentence structure. God knows that you are enough, knows you are in the process of a strategic purpose, and knows what that purpose is. It is just up to us to ask, seek, and knock.

QUESTIONS

The following are a few miraculous questions to get you started. If you would risk the conversation with the miraculous and surrender to a power outside yourself, I assure you the results will amaze you. In fact, I guarantee it.

1. In what areas of my life should I surrender control and trust that the miraculous will intervene on my behalf?

2. How has the miraculous been showing up in my life already that deserves my attention and, for whatever reason, I have failed to notice?

3. When would I be well served to listen to the miraculous rather than to intellectual reason tomorrow for a particular challenge or decision?

4. Are there certain areas in my life where the miraculous is answering my plea for clarity and where I have resisted listening?

5. How can I employ the miraculous in more of my business decisions to gain better clarity around circumstances that are beyond anyone's control?

6. The power of the miraculous is all around us. But noticing it is up to us. The resucceed system requires that you open yourself to the miraculous. Trust me, your life will never be the same.

QUICK TAKEAWAY

Is there an area of your life where you feel pushed instead of pulled? Open yourself to the miraculous for direction. Even if it is a big and important thing. Allow yourself access to the gift of the miraculous as a test, to ask, seek, and knock.

I am so excited to share with you the power of granular gratitude. It's easy to feel grateful for the big stuff, but finding it in the small stuff is resucceeding. That's what I share in the next chapter.

CHAPTER 21

GRANULAR GRATITUDE

Gratitude turns what we have into enough, and more. It turns denial into acceptance, chaos into order, confusion into clarity ... it makes sense of our past, brings peace for today, and creates a vision for tomorrow.

—MELODY BEATTIE

In my third year of undergraduate studies, I lived with a few guys in a house off campus. One afternoon, I had been playing loud music in my room when I emerged to grab something from the kitchen. I noticed that one of my roommates was sitting in the living room with two friends. I felt a little embarrassed about the volume of my music, so I went back to turn it down. As I passed the living room again, I looked at the two people sitting close together on the loveseat and talking with my roommate. The young woman was strikingly beautiful. She had a magnetic smile and kind eyes.

Instead of going to the kitchen again, I sat down on the hearth. I acted as if I wanted to hear their discussion. Really, I wanted only to watch the woman a little longer, to hear her laugh and see her smile. She was captivating. I could tell she was dating the guy sitting next to her based on their proximity, but I involved myself in the conversation and laughed when they laughed.

I'd been in a relationship of my own, which became a college engagement and then a college breakup. But I always remembered the woman on the loveseat and her smile. I'd see them around from time to time and had gotten to know the woman's boyfriend because we attended the same church.

After graduation, I stayed around for a few months while I figured out what I was going to do. One day while stepping into a crosswalk near campus, I saw the boyfriend. I waved to him, and right in the middle of the crosswalk, I stopped to ask a quick question. It was strange because we were standing in the middle of the street, but I knew this was my moment.

I had heard that he was leaving for a church mission in Russia for four years. I wondered if he would continue dating his girlfriend while he was away. So in the middle of the crosswalk, I asked him. It seemed like a reasonable question at the time.

"No," he said, "I don't feel that would fair to her, so we broke up."

With big smile, I raised my hand to shake his and wished him well on his mission trip. I'm fairly certain he could read my excitement.

Within a day, I was on the phone with his then ex-girlfriend, Maurita. Within two weeks, we met for a walk. Within four weeks, we were dating. And within two years, we were married. That was 21 years ago as I write this.

Fast-forward to the other day when I was practicing my ability to find gratitude in the small things, what I call granular gratitude. As part of my 5-Minute Epic Evening Ritual, I asked, what small events in my life seemed like coincidences at the time but deserve huge gratitude? The next morning during my Miracle Morning, when I came to my final re-affirm gratitude question, I immediately thought of how grateful I am for my wife. But, it was infinitely more powerful feeling grateful for the events that led to our getting together. For example, the fact that Maurita and her boyfriend were visiting with my roommate just as I needed something from the kitchen. Or that soon after this meeting, Maurita and I were in a human resources class together. Or that I ran into her boyfriend in the middle of the crosswalk a few weeks before I'd planned to move away from my college town.

When you find gratitude in the small things, you notice the miraculous alignment that has been working beneath the surface of your life. You begin to see your strategic purpose, your moments of brilliance, the miraculous events in your daily life: everything that has happened that you didn't orchestrate. There's nothing better than noticing what's great in your life that you didn't have to lift a finger to make happen, is there?

As a highly successful individual, you probably make a lot of things happen. If you're like me, you put your mind to a task, you discipline yourself, and after you've applied the required focused energy, you reap the fruits of your labor. You may even feel grateful for the ability to do all that.

When you shift your gratitude to those things you didn't make happen, you open yourself to the magic and mystery of forces beyond you.

A good example is that we rarely know why things are happening when we are in the middle of them, but as we get distance and look back, what seemed to be an uneven, zig-zagged road looks far more straight and predictable. As we improve our ability to seek those small events in our lives that are worthy of gratitude, we shorten the space and time required to look back and see the straighter, more predictable line. This is because we are shortening the time required to acknowledge the miraculous nature of the events and direction of our lives.

When I recall these occurrences, which originally seemed coincidental, I am moved to deep gratitude for them.

Here are a few things to remember when you practice gratitude for the small things.

1. GRATITUDE SHOULD MOVE YOU EMOTIONALLY.

It's so easy to treat gratitude as a process or an item on your to-do list instead of treating it as a gift. By opening yourself to the gift of gratitude, you will uncover amazing, yet small, moments in your life that you later realize were game changers. When certain moments happen, your life is never the same. A crosswalk experience, if you will. I am moved to tears sometimes when I uncover a small, seemingly insignificant moment in my life that is worthy of deep gratitude. Decide now that the way you find gratitude needs to go deep and move you emotionally. Decide now that you want to live in that state always. It's powerful.

2. GRATITUDE REQUIRES TRIGGERS.

It's great to set aside time to focus on gratitude. But remember gratitude is not a task; it's an ongoing part of your daily life.

Earlier, I mentioned my rule that I don't let my feet hit the carpet until I am moved to gratitude. This forces me to start my day from the perspective of being grateful. When I start my morning this way, gratitude follows me all day. In what areas of your life could you use gratitude? Is it when you pull into the garage at the end of your work day? Is it when you wake up? Is it right before you go to sleep? Is it when you turn a particular corner on the way to work? Is it whenever you see a couple holding hands? Creating triggers that remind you to feel gratitude allows it to become part of you. Initially it will feel contrived, but over time it becomes part of your daily life. Trigger it!

3. GRATITUDE IS TO BE SHARED.

You will find greater value in sharing gratitude with others. Even something personal can be a powerful way to connect with the people in your life. When I share the crosswalk story with others, they can't help but recall how small things have become major turning-points in their lives. When I am grateful for someone or something someone did for me, as I share that gratitude, I try to recall the smallest details, that little thing they did that altered my world or worldview.

For example, my teenage son just started driving. I'm grateful that he is being responsible with the car and his safety. But, if I go small with my gratitude, I am most thankful that he remembers to text his mom and I when he arrives at school and back home again. It warms my heart that he takes the time to text us. Each time it happens, I offer up gratitude. Find the small events in your life that make gratitude come alive.

The re-affirm question for granular gratitude is about locating seemingly insignificant, yet monumental, things to be grateful for. The 5-Minute Epic Evening Ritual helps you engage your creative mind through the subconscious and access to the miraculous. As you ask and receive answers, you expose areas of your life that deserve deep gratitude you've never considered.

QUESTIONS

Here are a few granular gratitude questions to try. As you develop your own list of opportunities for gratitude, I know your life story will change for the better.

1. What is something that has happened that changed my life's path and that I have always taken for granted or discounted as inconsequential or coincidental?

2. What is something small that [name of person] does for me that I have never recognized and that I can tell her or him about tomorrow?

3. What is something that causes stress and frustration in my life that deserves an equal amount of gratitude? Often your negative experiences shape your life or force

you to develop a skill or trait that now serves you more than it takes from you.

4. What are the big areas of gratitude in my life I should reinvestigate to uncover the smaller, more significant area of gratitude embedded within?

5. What are three key times within my normal business day when I can create compelling triggers to be grateful?

The fun starts when you no longer make broad sweeping statements of gratitude for the obvious stuff, like "I'm thankful for the roof over my head, the food on my table, the car that we drive, the vacations we get to go on." Don't get me wrong, it's important to be grateful for these things—not everyone in the world has access to them. But the small areas that deserve gratitude in your life create a massive amount of momentum. They are deeply meaningful because you didn't make them happen, and yet they often change the course of your life forever. Seek the small. In the end, it pays off big.

QUICK TAKEAWAY

What is something small that has happened in your life that you might have dismissed as a coincidence but that produced a major impact? It could be a person you met, a job you accepted, a phone call you received. Spend some time feeling the beauty of that opportunity that, having occurred, makes you feel well cared for, loved, and looked after. Give gratitude for this.

Do you celebrate your success or just move on to the next big adventure? In the next chapter, I impress upon you the need to schedule and insist on having celebratory moments throughout your life. To celebrate is to resucceed.

CHAPTER 22

CELEBRATION

When you jump for joy, beware that no one moves the ground from beneath your feet.

—STANISLAW JERZY LEC

As a type-A guy, it's been a challenge for me to take my hand off the proverbial plow, even for a second or two, to celebrate my successes. It's as if I'm worried that a celebration would detract from future achievement. Though probably written in jest, Stanislaw Jerzy Lec's quote above highlights my biggest fear: If I celebrate, I somehow risk the solid ground beneath my feet. The earth would simply fall away.

It turns out I'm not alone. I encounter plenty of people who struggle with this and fail to acknowledge their successes. When's the last time you scheduled time to celebrate your successes? I mean really celebrate. Businesses are known for year-end holiday parties or perhaps a launch party when a product is delivered, but in our quest or zeal, we defer, delay, or even detach from the art of celebration. In this desire for more, we miss the mysterious power of celebration.

As a sales guy, I used to say, "I'm only as good as my next deal." Shoot, you know my story: I couldn't even celebrate Christmas in 2006 as I sat agitated and stressed, hoping for one last deal, the deal that promised to demonstrate my worth and give me a good enough reason to celebrate.

When I look beyond myself to others, as I watch posts fly by on social media or even read of achievements in periodicals, I realize that we live in a world that rarely honors celebration outside of typical courtesy events that are imposed on us as tradition. Even then, are we celebrating or going through the motions? Many people I know work during holidays. We ask our family and friends to ignore our birthdays. We shy away from acknowledgement and accolades. In fact, if you think about it, many people view celebration as pompous in most circles, as if it breaks a credo or jinxes the possibility of future success.

In the chase for success and achievement, we don't dare consider celebrating. But what's the point of achievement if we can't enjoy it? Instead, we charge ahead, skipping the joy and hoping to rack up further successes. It's as if we believe that celebration would hamper our ability to succeed—in something we're good at—the next time, the next month, or year.

When will it be okay to celebrate?

What if we became great at celebrating the steps we take every day toward achievement of a goal? Celebration is as important to success as our effort. You deserve to stop and feel your success, not as pompous expression, but as acknowledgement and appreciation for not only achieving, but also being *ALIVE*.

What are the areas in your life that deserve this recognition that you have yet to celebrate? Where are you willing to let your success and achievement take on more meaning, fulfillment, and purpose? It is in celebrating your success that you acknowledge others for their contributions—the things they do to support your achievement. Your successes are the outward answer to your innermost questions. It surely deserves a day in the sun. I promise, you will be successful again, but take time to party.

The re-affirm celebration question allows you to pay homage to your success. Skipping this step cheapens it. You deserve to celebrate. Those who support and witness your success—family, friends, colleagues—deserve to celebrate along with you as well.

What if your goals included an element of celebration? When you set a goal, you dream, invent, and put forth effort, but as a part of that, you also plan to celebrate your realized goal. I believe your success and achievement would come alive with meaning and purpose. You would no longer be invisible, and survival success would dissipate as you celebrate each success.

Maurita and I came to the point with kids and assets when it was more than wise to hire a lawyer to help us draft a will. As part of that process, the attorney challenged us to consider many eventual possibilities we didn't want to think about. It's not surprising; wills deal with what would happen if we were no longer here. It was a strange process, like buying life insurance when you're grateful to make the investment for those you love, but bummed you wouldn't be with them if they had to make use of the money. I decided to make the will preparation process fun.

The attorney asked me what I wanted to happen when I die. I answered his questions, but then I said, in no uncertain terms, that I would not be okay with a memorial service. Instead, I required that a party, costing a minimum of $15,000, be thrown for my friends and family on Lake Union in Seattle to celebrate my life. I can still remember my wife looking at me as if I were crazy (as I knew she would be because she hates spending money).

My point is that it gives me a little peace knowing that my life will be punctuated by a party, not a sullen event where people fill out the guest book and act, dress, and look sad. The party is tentatively scheduled for soon after my death, whenever that is, and I love that. What will your party be like?

QUESTIONS

The following questions will help you begin celebrating. Take a close look at your life. Ask what areas deserve celebration and how you can incorporate it. This is the start of a whole new success experience for you. This is how you resucceed.

1. What areas of my life deserve celebration where I avoid it out of fear of future failure? (Hint: the smaller and more insignificant it seems the better.) As you get granular about celebration, you will resucceed.

2. Is there an easy way to modify my goals to include celebration that would foster a sense of fulfillment, meaning, and purpose in my success activities?

3. Is there someone at my work who deserves celebration for what they have brought that I haven't acknowledged?

4. What is one way I can institute a regular practice of celebrating my life regardless of achievement? (For simply being alive!)

5. How can I walk in daily celebration to model this for those I know and love and also show them the power of it?

QUICK TAKEAWAY

Think of a time when you celebrated and it felt great. Imagine that time. Ask yourself if that celebration took from you or gave to you. Record what you remember. When you've celebrated a win, has it ever interfered with your later success? Does jinxing count as a reason to not celebrate? When you incorporate celebration as a component of your success goals and rituals, you resucceed.

Hey, that's it. You've learned about what it means to resucceed and all about the great questions you can be asking just five minutes before you go to sleep with your 5-Minute Epic Evening Ritual. I hope that the context of these questions has opened you to the possibilities, to the questions that you have yet to know the answers to in your life and career. Just because the 5-Minute Epic Evening Ritual is simple doesn't mean it isn't transformational. Give it a try! Grab a stack of 3x5 cards. Write down your three great questions starting tonight. Resist the impulse to try to answer the questions you write down but instead allow your creative mind and the miraculous to go to work while you sleep. Let the resucceeding begin!

Next comes the epilogue of this book, which is all about unfinished nature of our lives. Although it might sound like a downer, it really isn't. Someday, we won't be here, but if we lived right, our work and impact is hardly finished. We live on through the unfinished melody that we create.

UNFINISHED MELODIES

I've told my children that when I die, to release balloons in the sky to celebrate that I graduated. For me, death is a graduation.

—ELISABETH KUBLER-ROSS

With all this talk about resucceeding and asking great questions, we must not forget the fleeting quality of life. Our time on earth is limited, and at some point our mortality will interrupt our plans. This shouldn't take away from resucceeding, but rather fuel the importance of it.

I would be doing you a disservice if I failed to encourage you to look at the end as you consider the resucceeding you plan to do while alive. Some of my best reflection has been done while pondering what would be important if I had only a few hours left. Such reflection might be frightening for some, but it is my hope that your mortality roots your determination even deeper and increases your zeal for meaning, purpose, and fulfillment. I urge you to find the time necessary to pause and reflect. Our mortality is our license and permission to live fuller lives.

What if I told you that your days are numbered but will not end? What if there is no finish line for you? That the checkered flag will not be waving, and you will not hear the roar of fans in the bleachers as you cross the line from life exuberant to death so quiet?

Regardless of your successes or achievements, your final day will come and go. But your story, magnified by your willingness to resucceed, will live on forever, like a well-loved song.

At age 53, Gene O'Kelly, the chief executive officer of the accounting firm KPMG, was told he would die in three months. He set out to write a book he had always dreamed of writing called *Chasing Daylight,* which the *New York Times* reviewer Janet Maslin called "a common-sense guidebook on how to die." In six short chapters, O'Kelly described what it is like to forego leaning on the past or future for direction, life purpose, meaning, fulfillment, and joy.

"[I]f you start to live in the present now," O'Kelly said, "not only do you get to enjoy it (which is huge), but you also prepare yourself for the future, which someday will be your present, breathing in your face. If you've practiced, you'll be able to live there. You'll have that muscle. It will be strong."

Chasing Daylight contains the spirit and heart for great questions: What if you were to stop relying on the past to dictate your future? What if you were open to a new design, a new story? The resucceed system challenges you to consider the possibility. To get out of your head and stop intellectualizing your next step. To be okay with the uncertainty of your life that, to date, has not been lived. To ask great questions instead of seeking to manufacture answers. That's what it means to resucceed, and it's available for you. Right now.

Merriam-Webster tells us that a melody is "a rhythmically organized and meaningful succession of single musical notes or tones having a definite relationship one with the other and forming an aesthetic whole." What if I told you that your life well lived is akin to the catchy melody of a great song? Even when the song is done, we remember the melody as we hum it through our day. Ever hear someone whistle the melody of a song and then hear that melody in your mind's ear? Even hours later, the whistler gone forever, that melody returns to visit you.

Such is true with your life, your success, your resucceeding. Our lives will most surely end with unfinished business. Undiscovered. Unopened. Unanswered. Unlived. *The unfinished melody continues.*

The music will fade for us all. First to dim, then only silence. But if we play this right, it's still there, waiting to be hummed or sung. As we resucceed, show up in our lives, ask great questions, and respond to the answers we receive, we become the unfinished melody that others will enjoy even once we've passed.

When I think about death, I'm reminded of my father's passing. Eighty-six years came down to just a few days as we waited patiently (or impatiently) for the silence to settle. In the antiseptic room of his care facility, I sat, listening to his labored breathing, noticing the metronome-like quality. A reminder that he was with me, but not for long. On the night his breathing went dim, I held his hand. That same strong, calloused hand, but this time I held his in mine.

I remembered his was the hand that held mine when he taught me how to fish and that swiftly grabbed the pole and gave it a quick tug to secure the fish once we had a nibble. His hands had made beautiful melodies playing the piano in our quiet house on a Sunday afternoon as I sat on the couch nearby trying to feel what he felt in the music. This hand had patted my back when I was sick and, later, built me a fort. The same hand wrote kind notes of encouragement during my first year in college.

Even though he couldn't move, I still sensed his presence. I cannot tell you how much I didn't want to let go, not that night and surely not for eternity.

The next day I returned, and the door to his room was closed. Not an exciting door to open, not one that whispered of opportunities. I was afraid of what I would find on the other side. When I entered, I heard the metronome of his breathing, though it was barely detectable. I held his hand again, and I could tell he was no longer with me. His hand felt empty. He was gone. But his melody, *oh his melody*, was still there. Perhaps even more than before. I no longer had the crutch of his physical presence. He had left a melody, and it was up to me to hum it on my own now.

I knew he would pass soon, but that didn't take anything from his story, his melody in my life and the lives of everyone he touched.

Many will say that death is the great equalizer of humanity, one thing we all have in common. But I say we all possess a melody that represents the life we've chased, dreamed of, created, and lived.

Years after my father died, in a car on a dusty road in Idaho, I sat with a new friend for several hours. Out of nowhere he asked a startling question, "Where are you at with dying?"

I stuttered a response, but I was far more interested in hearing his follow-up because I knew he was going somewhere.

"We are scared of dying," my friend explained, "only when we aren't taking the 'turns' that come our way while we are living."

His powerful and poignant words make me think of the voice I mentioned early in this book, heard at 2:00 a.m. when the house was quiet and still. The voice that challenged me to show up and respond to the call of my life. The call, our purpose, comprises the "turns" that come our way. My friend confirmed my thought that, as long as we take our turns and truly resucceed, we have no reason to fear death. We uncover what is behind our eyes and the reasons *behind the reasons* we do what we do. This is to take the turns that come our way. This is to resucceed.

Resucceeding gives us permission to avoid being consumed by things that don't really matter. Ending that human epidemic. We don't receive a guide book when we're born that tells us where to put our attention, what to focus on, and how to move beyond the minutia of life. We all share this poverty of spirit from time to time, and by our self-imposed preoccupation with the unessential, we remain numb to the important and transcendent that appears right in front of us. American journalist Sydney Harris said, "Regret for things we did can be tempered by time; it is regret for things we did not do that is inconsolable."

ENTER YOUR ROCKING CHAIR

Ever sat in a rocking chair? Many of us have inherited a rocking chair from someone who has since passed. Some of us buy rocking chairs as a symbol of relaxation, the good life. They make our houses look like home and harken to a different era when the pace of life allowed for more reflection, sipping lemonade, soft music, and the enjoyment of the simple things like sitting still. A rocking chair seems to whisper, "Sit with me and be okay with letting the day pass you by."

Consider this: Some people inhabit the world in a perennial race to the finish line, one that doesn't exist. Other people have learned or adopted the art of personal reflection. Which one resembles the life you live now? Do you possess the ability to achieve *and* reflect at the same time?

I'm not saying don't achieve or that you should abandon your competitive spirit or pursuit of excellence. I'm saying do not pursue success to the exclusion of what's essential, what makes you whole. The path to becoming someone who achieves and reflects is in learning to ask yourself tough questions and then listening for the answers.

Imagine yourself sitting in a rocking chair during the last years of your life. Ask yourself, what is most important to you? What is the present thread in your life that means the most to you? Engage in the struggle *now* with those big questions about who you are, who you are becoming, and why you do what you do. Let go of what keeps you up at night and instead discover what brings you lasting joy, peace, meaning, and fulfillment. This is to resucceed, which starts with being inquisitive and a belief in possibility.

You could dismiss this as optimistic chatter, better for another day or decade. I argue that this discipline will help you become more authentic. You will arrive in your own story without waiting for your final days and moments when life, *your life*, has passed you by. By asking tough questions about what is important to you, you become more yourself! I say again: You don't have to give up achievement to resucceed because you become more *your true self*. You become more approachable, achieve more, and invite more of what is most important.

I am not talking about a feeling here. I'm talking about answers to real questions. Clarity!

Take the rocking chair test. Close your eyes and imagine sitting in a rocking chair on your future covered porch in the final years of your life. Rock for a while, let the day pass, and watch the trees sway melodically in the breeze. At some point ask yourself, what matters to me now that I'm on the other side of _____? Then wait for your great answer. Watch the invisible become visible in your life.

This is resucceeding.

SPECIAL FREE BONUSES

5-MINUTE EPIC EVENING RITUAL

A Handy Reference for Those
Committed to Resucceeding

To download a comprehensive PDF of the entire 5-Minute Epic Evening Ritual, including sample questions, bedtime "ramp down" success routines, and tips and tricks, simply go to www.jamescolburn.net/resources.

FREE FAST LAUNCH PACKAGE

Give the Gift of Resucceeding

Many readers find the Resucceed system and the 5-Minute Epic Evening Ritual such a transformational process that they want to share it with those they love and care for. To help you help them, I have created what I call the "Free Fast Launch Package," which you can obtain by visiting www.jamescolburn.net/resources. By selecting the "Free Fast Launch Package," you can send your friends and loved ones the following for FREE:

- Three chapters of *Resucceed: Create an Extraordinary Future While You Sleep by Using the 5-Minute Epic Evening Ritual*

- FREE 5-Minute Epic Evening Ritual PDF Checklist

- FREE Training Videos and Audio on how to implement and immediately begin to Resucceed

I coach successful people to Resucceed. This is the answer to the call of my life. Each of us are called to fully "show up" in life with our unique brand and platform. My role in this is to help you bring forward hidden opportunities while exposing self-imposed limitations that hold you back. Seeing that light go on is my purpose. So much so, my logo is a light bulb.

All my coaching is done over the phone. This is by design to remove the typical obstacles to understanding. In most cases, you will never meet with me in person, which allows for a more meaningful, transparent coaching experience. Both coach and client find this helpful in the sharing and vulnerability that is necessary to resucceed.

I coach only highly successful, already-achieved individuals who seek to resucceed by adding fulfillment, meaning, passion, joy, and purpose to their lives.

Hire me when you seek one or more of the following:

- Emphatic desire to significantly increase your personal income

- Success that goes beyond what you have accepted and tolerated in your current brand of success

- Unquenchable interest in the 5-minute **Epic Evening Ritual** and how it can transform your life

- Profound new entrepreneurial startup that requires a new mindset and approach

- Energy management to get the most out of your work and play

- Clarification of purpose and strengths, and from this understanding, movement to the next level of success

My coaching clients have little to no patience for a long, drawn-out process, so my coaching agreements are never for longer than six months or more often than three times per month. My coaching clients come to me when they are absolutely ready to resucceed.

If you'd like to set up a personal 15 minute phone call with me, simply go to www.jamescolburn.net/coaching and follow the prompt to "Schedule a FREE 15-Minute Call." From there you will be directed to my scheduling application.

ACKNOWLEDGMENTS

Make sure at the very least you read the end of this section
because it's all about you, the reader.

The Acknowledgments are the very last pages of the book that I wrote and rightfully so. Honestly, I didn't even know where to start because there are so many people, both near and far, to whom I owe deep gratitude for the support, encouragement, and willing ears throughout the process of developing the content for this book. My sincere apologies to anyone I've missed here.

To God for always being there even when I was not, for your intangible love and the grace that covers my life, for the gift of your holy spirit and how you move in my life quietly and yet profoundly, and for challenging me to fully show up and to answer my call while here on earth, I thank you.

To Mom, my deep gratitude for all the hard work you did back in April of 1970. Your ever enthusiastic and constant optimism has been my inspiration in both the good and hard times of my life. Thanks for always believing in the best of me even when I doubted it.

Dad, I miss you so much, but I know you've been right by my side through this entire writing project. You taught me the gift of words and the wonder of bringing them to life in compelling ways to inspire those that read them. To have a dad who was an honorable man is a priceless gift. I am the man I am today because of you.

To my sisters Linda (#1) and Nancee (#1A), I can't tell you how lucky I am to have such independent souls for sisters. It is so cool to know that there are two others in the world that think and look at the world much the way I do. I appreciate each of you for your no BS views on life and your willingness to say it like it is.

To Maurita, my beautiful, brown-eyed, wonderfully pragmatic, patient, and giving (until it hurts sometimes) wife and mother of our three amazing children, I'm so grateful for our life together. Without your love and support, there would be no *Resucceed*. Proverbs 3:15 describes you and our life together best: "She is more precious than rubies; nothing you desire can compare with her." I love you so much, and I am so very happy you chose to love me back.

To my amazing kids, Eliot, Lucas, and Madeline, you guys make me look so good. You are bright, witty, caring, and compassionate, not to mention beautiful. Each page of *Resucceed* was influenced in one way or another by you. It is my hope and dream that your life will be filled with Resucceed moments. I love you more than I could ever attempt to write.

To Jennifer Reyer and David Wessling, I thank you from the bottom of my heart for your willingness to be my Resucceed guinea pigs over the years. Our friendship through this process has been invaluable. You know just the words to say and when to say them to keep me on course to completion.

To the many special people who allowed me to unpack and explore my emerging Resucceed content, I'm grateful for your trust and support: Forrest Inslee, my entire grad school "Cohort #5," Verlon and Melodee Fosner, Todd Aagard, Rick Justus, Peter Hickey, Laurie Zaleski, Rod Watson, Omeed Salashoor, Bruce Rodich, Chris Peppler, DJ and Jenny Vick, Cary Peterson, Ryan Riley, Ron and Linda Ruthruff, Jeff Ericson, David Carlson, Brian Clark, Andy Ferguson, Martin Barrett, Isaac Stegman, and the list surely goes on and on.

To my amazing writing editor and confidant, Leslie Watts, as Jerry McGuire uttered in the movie of the same name, "You complete me." And surely you did on this project. I thank you for climbing in my head and helping me get the essence of what I was trying to say on paper. I am sure that once I knew I had you as backup, I could actually finish this book.

To the mentors, teachers, and authors who inspired me to think on my own, to dream the best for others, and to let go of the limiting beliefs that held me back, I thank you for echoing in the world: To Craig Sigl, Scott Gallagher, Mark Smith, Tony Robbins, Dave Ramsey, Dan Harris, Jeff Goins, Rudy Herr, Vern Holden, James Allen, Norman Doidge, Gene O'Kelly, Tim Marusich, Jeffrey Townsend, Hal Elrod, Richard Rohr, Robert Fulghum, Parker Palmer, Michael Cole, Viktor Frankl, Dan Kennedy, Maxwell Maltz, Gary Keller, David Platt, William Donius, T.D. Jakes, Steven Pressfield, Chris Ihrig, Jon Courson, Alan Boehmer, Brennan Manning, Francis Chan, Marcus Buckingham, and Brené Brown. A notable thank you to Amanda Murphy, the coach of a lifetime, for our brief but transformational work together on playing Legos, realizing that fear is a negative fuel, living a "million-dollar life," and designing what it means to be fully alive and compassionate. I owe you a great deal of gratitude for the influence and impact that you contributed to my life. And to think, we never once met in person!

To my private coaching clients, sharing in your life and watching each of you grow, expand, and answer the call of your life is such a gift. Be assured that we are learning in equal measure during our time together and that your choice to entrust me to help you with your Resucceed adventure is an honor and privilege I do not take lightly.

To everyone that supported the launch of this book, for those who weighed in on the book cover and read early versions of the book, I give my hearty thanks for your precious and selfless feedback to help me produce a meaningful and easy-to-read book. To those that pass the book along to anyone and everyone you know, I appreciate your spreading the word. And to all those that have chosen to write a review on Amazon and elsewhere, thank you for helping others find this book.

Finally, to you the reader, thank you for allowing this book into your life and for giving the 5-Minute Epic Evening Ritual a try. Thanks for all your support and feedback in the Resucceed Community on Facebook. Thank you for making it possible for me to continue producing this book, to give it away as often as I can, and to continue to donate to the amazing work and mission of the Family Lines and Medical Teams International organizations. If there is anything I can do to support you, the causes that you support, or to simply lend a helping hand, I'd love for you to contact me.

To connect with me, follow @james_colburn on Twitter, Facebook.com/james.colburn on Facebook, or join the Resucceed Community on Facebook www.theresucceedcommunity.com. Or, go to www.jamescolburn.net to visit my website.

Remember, it all starts with asking a few great questions. Truly, the better we get at asking great questions, the better our lives will become.

ABOUT THE AUTHOR

JAMES COLBURN has worked for more than two decades in executive and entrepreneurial roles in marketing, real estate, nonprofits, and consulting. Along the way, his experience revealed to him the trap of success: After becoming his company's top performer in sales, breaking records, and selling tens of millions of dollars' worth of real estate each year, he came to understand that conventional measures of achievement can keep even the best performers from finding fulfillment. He wrote *Resucceed: Create an Extraordinary Future While You Sleep by Using the 5-Minute Epic Evening Ritual* to share his insights with others so that they can fulfill their own potential.

James has a bachelor's degree from the University of Oregon in Business, and a master's degree in International Community Development from the College of Social and Behavioral Sciences at Northwest University. He and his wife, Maurita, are active in charitable work focused on families and global health. James serves as a guest lecturer in the School of Global Studies at Northwest University. He lives with his wife and three children in the Seattle area.

To contact James about media appearances, speaking at your event, or if you want to receive free training videos and resources, visit www.jamescolburn.net. To connect with James on social media, follow @james_colburn on Twitter, Facebook.com/james.colburn on Facebook, or join the Resucceed Community on Facebook, www.theresucceedcommunity.com.

For bulk order discounts of *Resucceed* or other books written by James Colburn, please go to www.jamescolburn.net/book.

A SPECIAL INVITATION TO JOIN THE RESUCCEED COMMUNITY

Like-minded fans and readers of *Resucceed* make up the extraordinary community that has put to work the daily transformational practice of the 5-Minute Epic Evening Ritual. As the creator of the Resucceed success ritual, I feel it is my responsibility to create and maintain an online opportunity to share, connect, and engage as a community with those who have learned and benefited from the art and design of asking great questions just five minutes before bedtime.

It is my hope and dream that those who find the Resucceed 5-Minute Epic Evening Ritual beneficial will become members of our growing community to inspire and support one another and provide accountability within the online community for transformational growth.

Just go to Facebook and type "The Resucceed Community" (or visit www.theresucceedcommunity.com) and request to join the Resucceed Community on Facebook®. There you will be able to connect with like-minded individuals who are in the process of practicing the Resucceed success ritual.

I'll be moderating the Resucceed Community on Facebook personally and checking in regularly to provide feedback, encouragement, and support. It is my honor to be a part of the Resucceed Community.

If you'd like to connect with me personally on social media, follow @James_Colburn on Twitter and Facebook.com/james. colburn on Facebook. Please feel free to send me a direct message, leave a comment, or ask me a question. I do my best to respond to each message. Let's connect soon!

If you'd like to set up a personal 15 minute phone call with me, simply go to www.jamescolburn.net/coaching and follow the prompt to "Schedule a FREE 15-Minute Call." From there you will be directed to my scheduling application.